3-31-75

Industrial Concentration and
Economic Power in Pakistan

Lawrence J. White

Industrial Concentration and Economic Power in Pakistan

Princeton University Press
Princeton, New Jersey

LCC: 73-2493
ISBN: 0-691-04197-0

Library of Congress Cataloging in Publication Data
will be found on the last printed page of this book

Publication of this book has been aided by the
Whitney Darrow Publication Reserve Fund.

This book has been composed in Linotype Times Roman

Printed in the United States of America
by Princeton University Press, Princeton, New Jersey

This book is dedicated to

Shelley,

whose idea it all was in the first place

Contents

Tables

Preface

THE ideas behind this book originated in 1969, when my
wife and I were working as economists for the Harvard
Development Advisory Service in Pakistan. The old government of Ayub Khan had been deposed, and the new
government of Yahya Khan was in power. Criticisms of
the former regime were widespread, and reformist ideas
and proposals were being encouraged by the new government. One of the major issues under discussion was the
problem of "the twenty-two families" or the "monopolies"
problem. My wife suggested that, since my training was
in industrial organization, I could probably make a productive contribution to the discussion. Unfortunately,
the press of other work at the time and an unexpected
transfer to Indonesia prevented very much immediate
work on the problem. My interest in the problem remained, however, and after our return to the United States
I began seriously to pursue research on the topic. This
book is the final product of that research.

I owe a debt of gratitude to a number of institutions
and individuals: the American Council of Learned So-
cieties, for providing the main financial support of the
research; the Research Program in Economic Development of the Woodrow Wilson School at Princeton, for
providing general facilities support and summer support
during the actual writing of the manuscript; the Harvard

Development Advisory Service, in whose employ I was when these ideas originated, and at whose conference in Torremolinos, Spain, in September 1972 I presented many of the ideas in this book and received many valuable comments; Lester Gordon, Edward S. Mason, Stephen R. Lewis, Jr., Gordon Winston, Shane Hunt, and Sherman Robinson, all of whom carefully read the manuscript at earlier stages and offered valuable suggestions and encouragement; Priscilla Read and Douglas Noll, who assisted in data collection and computations; and Mrs. Dorothy Rieger, who superintended the typing of the various drafts of the manuscripts.

Lawrence J. White
Princeton University

Industrial Concentration and
Economic Power in Pakistan

Chapter 1

Introduction

WITHIN a few weeks of taking office, Pakistan's President
Z. A. Bhutto, in January 1972, "nationalized" ten industries in Pakistan and placed under house arrest two of
the leading Pakistani industrialists.[1] Both actions were
somewhat symbolic: the government already controlled
a number of the firms in these industries and it only appointed new managers for the remaining firms, while
allowing the ownership of the assets to remain with the
original owners; the two industrialists were released
shortly afterwards. But the actions were taken in response to a real political problem within Pakistan. A
comparative handful of family groups dominate the industrial structure of Pakistan. The perceived economic
power and income distribution effects of this domination
have generated widespread political concern.

This book offers an analysis of the problems of industrial concentration and industrial economic power in
Pakistan. The framework is largely the industrial organization methodology, with suitable modifications, that
has been developed for analyzing developed economies.
The book limits itself to Pakistan, but I believe that the
concepts, methods, findings, and policies discussed have
widespread applicability for less developed countries
generally.

[1] *New York Times*, January 3, 1972, p. 1.

Studies of industrial organization have traditionally confined themselves to the advanced countries of the West. This is not surprising since, until recently, this is where virtually all of the industry was. These studies have concerned themselves primarily with the structural characteristics of individual markets, the behavior of firms in those markets, and the consequent performance of the firms judged against some criteria.[2] The primary welfare concerns of these studies are the efficient allocation of resources in a static sense and the dynamic improvement in productivity and product over time.

As less developed countries (LDC's) have created fledgling industrial structures, the concepts of industrial organization have become relevant for these countries. Yet, only Bain[3] and Merhav[4] have attempted general industrial organization approaches that deal with LDC's. There has not yet been a complete industrial organization study of the industrial sector of an individual LDC. It is the major thesis of this book that industrial organization tools—with some modification—provide a useful framework for analyzing an important set of LDC problems.

Most of the traditional studies of industrial organization have neglected questions concerning the overall concentration of economic power. This problem is some-

[2] Good summaries of current industrial organization methodology are found in the following texts: Joe S. Bain, *Industrial Organization*, 2nd edn. (New York, 1968); Richard E. Caves, *American Industry: Structure, Behavior, Performance*, 3rd edn. (Englewood Cliffs, 1972); and F. M. Scherer, *Industrial Market Structure and Economic Performance* (Chicago, 1970).

[3] Joe S. Bain, *International Differences in Industrial Structure* (New Haven, 1966).

[4] Meir Merhav, *Technological Dependence, Monopoly, and Growth* (New York, 1969).

times mentioned, but analytical models are less well developed and bases for welfare judgments are less clear than for the study of concentration in individual markets. However, many LDC's find the question of the concentration of economic power is exceedingly troublesome; Pakistan is not unique in this respect. Hazari[5] and Kothari[6] have made attempts to identify and quantify industrial control patterns in India. "Who Owns Kenya?" was the title and subject of a study in that East African country.[7] Many Latin American countries are concerned about ownership patterns and, in particular, foreign ownership patterns.[8] This study, besides providing estimates of the extent of the concentration of industrial economic power in Pakistan, will try to offer a framework for understanding how and why such concentrations can arise and what their economic and non-economic effects are likely to be.

Pakistan, though, is fairly unique (this would also apply to India) in that foreign ownership is not important economically or politically. Thus, a discussion of the problem of overall concentration is somewhat easier, since one does not have to deal with the very emotionally

[5] E. K. Hazari, *The Corporate Private Sector* (Bombay, 1966).

[6] M. L. Kothari, *Industrial Combinations* (Allahabad, 1967).

[7] National Christian Council of Kenya, *Who Owns Kenya?* (Nairobi, 1968).

[8] See Ricardo Lagos, *La Concentracion del Poder Economico* (Santiago, 1962); Frank Brandenburg, *The Development of Latin American Private Enterprise* (Washington, D.C., 1964); Carlos Malpica, *Los Dueños del Peru*, 3rd edn. (Lima, 1968); and Shane Hunt, "Distribution, Growth, and Government Economic Behavior in Peru," in *Government and Economic Development*, Gustav Ranis, ed. (New Haven, 1971).

charged question of foreign ownership. For better or for worse, Pakistanis own Pakistani industry.[9]

This study focuses on Pakistan before it broke up into Pakistan (West) and Bangladesh. A good deal of the analysis centers on 1968 and the years immediately preceding. There are a number of major reasons for doing this. First, at the time of writing, some of the important industrial data are available only up through 1968. The disruptions and splitting of the country have made further data collection difficult. Second, 1968 was really the last "typical" year for Pakistan. Early 1969 saw a wave of strikes and disorders that finally brought down the Ayub Khan government. The elections and the severe typhoon in the east in 1970 make that year atypical. And 1971, of course, saw eight months of severe disruption in the east and the final dismemberment of the country. The data that are used and the conclusions reached mean more if one is analyzing a typical year rather than one in which the economy (and country) was disintegrating.

Third, 1968 was the year in which the monopoly and ownership concentration question became a serious political issue. If one tried to put together ownership patterns for a later year, one might discover that some of the groups had started to cover their tracks. This was not yet likely in 1968. Finally, important parts of the analysis below rely on data taken from the balance sheets of firms listed on the Karachi Stock Exchange. In 1969 (the most recent year for which complete compiled data are available) many of these firms changed their accounting year. For accounting year 1969, some firms reported results

[9] One of the complaints of the Bengalis of East Pakistan, though, was that most of the industry there was "foreign owned" by West Pakistani industrialists.

for only six months and others reported results for as long as eighteen months. Correcting for these differences would have been extremely difficult, if not impossible. The figures for 1968 posed few such problems. Despite the absence of up-to-the-minute figures, I believe that this study retains its usefulness for its insights into an important set of problems that confronted Pakistan in the 1960's and that will continue to confront Pakistan and Bangladesh, along with many other LDC's, in the 1970's and 1980's. This book has little to say on the question of the splitting off of Bangladesh from Pakistan. To the extent that the industrial concentration worsened income distribution generally, and to the extent that the Bengalis resented the "foreign" ownership of East Pakistan industry by West Pakistan industrialists and resented having to buy overpriced West Pakistani manufactured goods, the industrial policies may have contributed to the ultimate Bangladesh split, but I do not think they were crucial. Different policies by the Central Government between 1950 and 1971 might have avoided the split and still could have been economically and politically compatible with the industrial concentration and industrial economic power pattern that existed.

Finally, I should make it clear that this study is not intended to cast blame on anyone or try to find out who was responsible. During the middle 1960's, Pakistan was considered by many to be a success story in terms of economic development and especially rapid industrialization. Only in 1969 did the cracks in the plaster appear and the economy and the politics of the country become unstuck. With the power of hindsight, many observers afterward realized that perhaps Pakistan's performance and policies had not been so good after all, but few thought so at the time.[10] One certainly cannot fault the Pakistani industrialists for taking advantage of the opportunities open to them. That is exactly what was expected of them. If the consequences were unfortunate, it was up to the people of Pakistan, through one means or another, to change the rules.

The Organization of this Book

Chapter 2 defines terms and reviews the analytics of industrial structure, keeping in sight the problem of LDC's. Special attention is given to the concept of barriers to entry in an LDC context. The economic and non-economic effects of industrial concentration and overall economic power are discussed. Chapter 3 presents a brief review of the Pakistani industrial experience, to set the scene for what follows.

Chapter 4 provides estimates of the overall concentration of economic power in the manufacturing sector of Pakistan. Though this has come to be known as the problem of "the twenty-two families," the estimates include a wider group. The sources, methods, and limitations on these estimates are discussed and some temporal and international comparisons provided. Concentration in banking and insurance is analyzed.

Industrial concentration in individual markets is the subject of Chapter 5. Although an industrial census to provide concentration figures for Pakistan is not available, relevant figures have been gathered from enough sources so that a reasonably complete picture of indus-

[10] There were two notable exceptions. See John H. Power, "Industrialization in Pakistan: A Case of Frustrated Take-Off?" *Pakistan Development Review* (Summer 1963) and Keith B. Griffen, "Financing Development Plans in Pakistan," *Pakistan Development Review* (Winter 1965).

trial concentration can be drawn. The qualifications and limitations to these figures are discussed and an international comparison offered.

Chapter 6 discusses the origins of both kinds of concentration found in the previous two chapters. Primary emphasis is given to the barriers to entry created by Pakistan's intensive system of investment and trade controls. Chapter 7 then analyzes some of the economic and noneconomic effects that both kinds of concentration created. A model of profit rates is constructed and tested. Industrial growth rates are examined. Political power and income distribution consequences are detailed.

Finally, Chapter 8 discusses the general sorts of policies that could be used to deal with concentration problems and reviews the policies that Pakistan has in fact pursued.

Chapter 2

The General Problem

The Relevance of the Industrial Sector

AT the beginning, one has to ask why anyone should really care about what happens in the industrial sector of the economy of LDC's. This might appear to be a foolish question, since most of the economic policies of LDC's over the past twenty years have been aimed at creating an industrial sector, and much scholarly time and effort has recently been devoted to analyzing the trade and protection policies of LDC's that have been designed to encourage industry.[1] Yet, the industrial sector is comparatively small in most LDC's. Many of these countries are still predominantly agricultural. Outside of Latin America, value added in manufacturing typically accounts for only 10%-15% of GNP, and it employs only 5%-10% of the labor force. By contrast, agriculture typically accounts for about half of GNP and two-thirds to three-fourths of the labor force. In Pakistan, value added in mining and manufacturing contributed only 11% to GNP in 1968, and these sectors employed roughly 8% of the labor force. In comparison, agriculture contributed 46.2% to GNP and absorbed over 70%

[1] A useful summary of many of these studies is contained in Ian Little, Tibor Scitovsky, and Maurice Scott, *Industry and Trade in Some Developing Countries* (London, 1970).

of the labor force. "Large scale" manufacturing[2] by itself contributed only 8.2% to GNP and employed only 1.6% of the labor force. Is manufacturing really worth worrying about? The answer is "yes" for three important reasons. First, most LDC governments have pinned their long-run hopes on the industrial sector. Although many governments have recently come to realize that improving the technology in agriculture probably offers the best way of immediately raising incomes for a large proportion of their populations, still, in the long run, improved agricultural technology will mean that resources can be released from agriculture and will have to be absorbed elsewhere in the economy. Manufacturing is the prime candidate. It is also the symbol of modernization. Manufacturing is identified with the high incomes of North America, Western Europe, the Soviet Union, and Japan. In manufacturing lie the long-run hopes and aspirations of most LDC governments. To the extent that current patterns of manufacturing affect future patterns, they are worth worrying about.

Second, the manufacturing sector interacts with other sectors in the economy. It buys raw materials and services inputs from other sectors, and it sells intermediate inputs to other sectors. Further, trade and exchange rate policies (e.g., import substitution policies) that benefit the manufacturing sector will implicitly or explicitly affect other sectors in the economy (e.g., agricultural exporting sectors). Thus, distortions in the manufacturing sector can have serious ramifications for other sectors.

[2] In Pakistan, this included all firms with 20 employees or over and all firms using power.

Third, many LDC governments are urban-based and responsive to their urban constituencies. Manufacturing is an urban phenomenon; manufacturing activities tend to be established where people already are, and the establishments themselves help create urban environments by attracting workers and attendant services to places where they had not previously been. The urban population is usually aware of the activities and actions of the manufacturing sector, and forms opinions about these actions which can be influential in shaping government policies. The industrialists themselves will be an important part of the constituency that tries to influence policy. Hence, the shape and pattern of the manufacturing sector may be disproportionately important in affecting government policies. A good example of this phenomenon is the concern within LDC's about income distribution. It generally seems to be the urban working and middle classes (themselves quite well off compared to the bulk of the rural population) who are most acutely aware of the income disparities created by manufacturing profits and who try to influence government policies to correct these disparities.

What happens in industry, then, matters. It is the thesis of this study that industrial concentration and industrial economic power also matter. The remainder of this chapter is organized as follows: The first section defines the important industrial organization terms used in the remainder of the study. Then, the simple analytics of monopoly and barriers to entry are reviewed in the context of LDC economies; this is followed by a review of the dynamic effects of monopoly. Next, the wider social and political consequences of monopoly power are developed, with a subsequent discussion of monopoly, profits, income distribution, and growth in LDC's. Finally, the wider problem of the concentration of economic power is discussed.

Defining Terms

Defining some terms at this point should help the exposition that follows. By "industrial concentration," I mean some measure of the number and/or relative sizes of firms within a single reasonably well-defined industry or market. An industry with high concentration would be one in which a few firms controlled a large percentage of the economic activity in that industry. The fewer the firms in the industry and the more openly and easily they can coordinate their actions, the more likely they are to achieve results similar to those of a monopoly.[3] In the pages that follow, my references to "monopoly" also mean oligopolies that can coordinate well enough so as to approximate monopoly results.

By "concentration of economic power," or concentration in the large, I mean some measure of the total assets or economic activity in the entire economy or in some broad sector of it that are owned or controlled by a number of identifiable groups or organizations. The primary focus will be on the concentration of economic power in the manufacturing sector. High concentration, then, would mean a relatively few individuals or organizations owning or controlling a large percentage of the assets or sales of the entire manufacturing sector.

Monopoly-oligopoly and overall industrial economic

[3] See Edward H. Chamberlin, *The Theory of Monopolistic Competition*, 8th edn. (Cambridge, Massachusetts, 1962), and William Fellner, *Competition Among the Few* (New York, 1949).

power concentration frequently go hand-in-hand in LDC's. Their industrial sectors are comparatively small and do not show the full diversification of a Western industrial country. A few monopolies or oligopolies in large industries may well account for a large share of the assets of the entire industrial sector. But the two problems are not necessarily linked, and they need to be analyzed separately. That overall ownership concentration need not be associated with monopoly-oligopoly can be shown by the following example. If only 100 groups or families owned or controlled all of the industrial assets of a country, overall concentration of industrial economic power would be high. Yet, if each group had a company producing and selling in each industrial market and the 100 companies were of roughly equal size, this market structure might well yield results that were close to those of a perfect competition model.

Monopoly and Barriers to Entry

The static allocative effects of a monopoly are well known and are as relevant to LDC's as to developed countries; a monopoly tends to charge a higher price and produce a lower output than would a group of perfect competitors facing the same circumstances. The monopolist thereby generates excess profits for himself. The welfare implications of this monopoly outcome have become somewhat ambiguous since the development of the "general theory of second best."[4] In a world with many imperfections and distortions, one can no longer be sure of the welfare effect of any simple distortion. The best that can be said is that a monopoly decreases social welfare if the resources that are released by the reduced out-

[4] See R. G. Lipsey and K. Lancaster, "The General Theory of the Second Best," *Review of Economic Studies* (1956-1957).

put are absorbed by sectors that have a smaller percentage spread between price and social marginal cost.[5] A second allocative effect is the "X-inefficiency" created by the lack of competitive pressure on the monopolist to minimize his costs. If one of the pleasures of monopoly is "the quiet life," the monopolist might not attain the technologically feasible minimum costs that competition might otherwise force on him.[6] By using inefficiently too many resources (for his too small output), he may be sharing his monopoly profits but he is depriving the economy of additional goods and services. Unfortunately, these costs are frequently overlooked or sometimes even applauded in LDC's. Governments in LDC's frequently have the goal of maximizing the domestic value added of existing production processes. The "quiet life" monopolist may well achieve this goal. But to the extent that the factors of production going into domestic value added have alternative uses, this goal can be quite costly.

Further, there is some evidence that a firm with a monopoly or market power position may choose capital-intensive technologies that are inappropriate for LDC's.[7]

[5] Social welfare is measured here by the familiar consumers' surplus triangle. In some writings the spread between price and social marginal cost is the "degree of monopoly power," but it could also be caused by externalities or "quiet life" X-inefficiencies. See Harvey Leibenstein, "Allocative Efficiency vs. X-Efficiency," *American Economic Review* (June 1966). For a more complete discussion of the static allocative effects of monopoly, and its qualifications, see F. M. Scherer, *Industrial Market Structure and Economic Performance*, pp. 12-27.

[6] Leibenstein, *op.cit.*

[7] Louis T. Wells, Jr., "Economic Man and Engineering Man: Choice of Technology in a Low Wage Country," mimeo, Harvard Development Advisory Service (Cambridge, 1972).

Freed from the cost-minimizing pressures of competition, a monopolist may choose the "easy" technology of high capital intensity, thereby freeing himself from the difficulties of managing a large number of workers and also earning for himself the prestige of ownership of a bright, shiny, "modern" automated factory. If he were pressed by competition, he might well make a different choice.

An oligopoly market structure may not change these conclusions very much. As mentioned above, the greater the ease with which rivals can come together to agree on common price and product strategies, the closer they will come to the monopoly outcome. Most countries, LDC's included, do not have the political and legal traditions of antitrust found in the United States. The legal barriers to oligopolistic coordination are much weaker or non-existent. For industries with more than a few members, trade associations (which are as common in LDC's as they are in developed countries) may serve as the vehicle for collusive agreements. LDC governments, in the interests of domestic price stability or of maximizing foreign exchange earnings, often encourage producers to come together and fix prices.

For a monopolist-oligopolist to continue enjoying the economic fruits of his position, there must be some barriers to entry into the industry at the production stage and marketing stage. Otherwise new firms would enter the industry at the production stage or at the marketing stage (via imports) and compete away the high profits. The LDC landscapes are usually covered with such barriers, both natural and artificial.

Bain has identified three types of barriers at the production stage:[8] (1) economies of scale, (2) control of

[8] Joe S. Bain, *Barriers to New Competition* (Cambridge, Massachusetts, 1956).

scarce factors, and (3) absolute capital requirements. The first of Bain's production barriers means that a new entrant must gain a significant share of the market to produce efficiently. A new entrant cannot slip unnoticed into an industry and thus face the unpleasant choice of overcrowding the industry and inviting retaliation by the existing members of the industry or of entering at a smaller, less obtrusive scale but with higher production costs. The second barrier means that existing firms may have special access to scarce factors of production. New entrants can obtain these scarce factors only at increasing costs and hence are at a relative disadvantage. The third means that the amount of capital required for entry, compared to the amounts that are normally lent in the capital markets and in the light of the perceived risks, may make financing and hence entry difficult and costly for potential entrants.

To this list I would add a fourth barrier, at the marketing stage: (4) tariffs and licenses on competing imports. Barriers at both the production and marketing stage are necessary for monopoly profits to persist. If there were only production barriers, imports would enter the country from efficient producers abroad; only the "natural" tariff of transport costs would provide any monopoly profits.[9] If there were only marketing barriers—import tariffs and licenses creating high domestic prices and potentially high profits—domestic firms would enter the industry and continue to do so until the super-normal profits disappeared.

All four categories of barriers are relevant for LDC's. Many of the barriers have been created by LDC government policies. In their efforts to industrialize, many LDC

[9] For non-transportable services, the natural tariff is infinite, so production barriers are sufficient to create monopoly profits.

governments have maintained overvalued exchange rates, with consequent foreign exchange licensing and rationing. Imported capital goods, spare parts, and raw materials are available at favorable exchange rates and low tariffs, but only to holders of import licenses. Simultaneously, consumption goods are imported at unfavorable exchange rates and high tariffs or often are subject to outright bans. Consequently, those who have access to the capital goods and raw materials licenses have highly profitable markets for which they can produce.

The tariffs and quotas on the finished goods provide a marketing barrier. Simultaneously, the licenses on the capital goods and raw materials create a scarce resource barrier. These licenses are indeed a scarce resource, as is indicated by the black-market prices for foreign exchange that exceed the official rate and by the high markups that holders of these licenses receive when they sell their goods.[10]

Import licensing as a means of rationing foreign exchange (as opposed to tariffs or a devaluation) usually has three justifications related to production decisions:[11]

[10] For the Pakistani evidence on this, see Mati Lal Pal, "The Determinants of the Domestic Price of Imports," *Pakistan Development Review* (Winter 1964); Mati Lal Pal, "Domestic Prices of Imports in Pakistan, Extension of Empirical Findings," *Pakistan Development Review* (Winter 1965); Mohiuddin Alamgir, "The Domestic Prices of Imported Commodities in Pakistan: A Further Study," *Pakistan Development Review* (Spring 1968); and A. I. Aminul Islam, "An Estimation of the Extent of Overvaluation of the Domestic Currency in Pakistan at the Official Rate of Exchange, 1948/49–1964/65," *Pakistan Development Review* (Spring 1970).

[11] There are two other justifications frequently given for import licensing, especially for consumer goods: (1) Even very high tariffs will not choke off import demand; this is based on

(1) government bureaucrats genuinely feel that they can allocate resources better than can existing markets; (2) licensing allows the "little man" a break, gives him access to licenses, and prevents him from being swept aside in the market by the more powerful "big men"; in theory, then, it is an encouragement rather than a barrier to entry; and (3) licensing provides an extra economic incentive—a favorable exchange rate for imported inputs —to spur investment and entrepreneurial activity.

Many bureaucrats think of unregulated competitive markets as destructive and wasteful of economic resources.[12] They are no doubt encouraged in this view by those who would otherwise be subjected to the rigors of competition. On the other hand, bureaucrats recognize that unregulated monopolies will also lead to undesirable results, and many LDC bureaucrats see the markets of their countries as shot through with monopolistic imperfections. The "natural" way out is for the bureaucracy to influence the allocation of resources, so as to soften the apparent anti-social effects of competition and monopoly. That this course of action also heightens the power and importance of the bureaucracy is a nontrivial side effect. Whether the resulting allocation of resources is better depends on the goals that have been

---

a belief that demand curves are perfectly inelastic or nearly so. (2) Licensing, along with a low exchange rate, will keep the prices of imported goods low; implicit here is the belief (or hope) that the recipients of these licenses will not take advantage of their scarcity value. The evidence accumulated by Alamgir indicates that this latter belief has not been justified in Pakistan. Wholesale mark-ups have been considerably higher on licensed goods with low tariffs than on those goods with high tariffs or those which were freely importable with more costly bonus vouchers. See Alamgir, *op.cit.*

[12] E. K. Hazari, *The Corporate Private Sector*, p. 359.

established. Little, Scitovsky, and Scott have surveyed the growth and welfare effects of this method of allocation.[13] The discussion of the other two justifications for licensing can shed some further light on this point. The actual practice of import licensing is usually just the opposite of the "little man equity" argument.[14] Licensing schemes usually have some explicit "historical shares" or "capability" basis. Even where these are not explicit, they are safe guidelines for a bureaucrat who is interested in minimizing the risk of something unexpected happening or in making sure that the licensed materials are not wasted. And it is the "big men," the large, well-established firms, who usually have the largest historical shares and who seem the most competent and capable.

[13] I. Little, T. Scitovsky, and M. Scott, *op.cit.*

[14] There is mounting evidence on this point. The Pakistani evidence will be presented in Chapter 7, below. For India, see Carl H. Fulda and Irene Till, "Concentration and Competitive Potential in India," *The Antitrust Bulletin* (Fall 1968); for Colombia, see Carlos F. Diaz-Alejandro, "The Mechanisms for Containing Imports: The System During 1971 and a Retrospective Look at Its Evolution (Import Controls)," Center Discussion Paper No. 158, Yale University Economic Growth Center (September 1972), pp. 28-32. Ranis has noted that East Pakistan tended to receive a larger fraction of the total imports into Pakistan when the import regime was liberalized than when imports were more tightly licensed. See Gustav Ranis, "Review of Books by Lewis and MacEwan," *Journal of International Economics* (May 1972). Along similar lines, Killick has noted that direct price controls on commodities in Ghana, though nominally intended to help the poor and the lower classes, were effectively enforced only in those areas where the urban upper middle class shopped and on those items which they primarily bought. See Anthony J. Killick, "Price Controls, Inflation, and Income Distribution: The Ghanaian Experience," mimeo, presented at the Torremolinos Conference of the Harvard Development Advisory Service (September 1972).

The large firm is better known to the bureaucrats of the licensing agency; it knows the ropes. Person-to-person relationships may be established. By contrast, a small firm or newcomer frequently appears risky and less competent. It is less well known to the bureaucrats. It may frequently be unfamiliar with the proper procedures to follow. It may even be unaware of particular licensing opportunities.

As a consequence, the large, well-established, monopolistic-oligopolistic companies frequently receive and continue to receive all or most of the licenses and continue to maintain their historical shares and their apparent competence. The process is self-reinforcing. A scarce resource barrier is created.

The same description and result would apply to the distribution of subsidized investment loans by LDC governments. Again, the price is usually too favorable, and the supply has to be administratively rationed. And, again, it is the large monopolistic-oligopolistic companies who are the recipients of the loans. The same story often holds for the letting of government contracts. In cases where competitive bidding is not required, or even where it is but quality factors dominate and subjective judgment by the government bureaucrats is necessary, the large companies will come out far ahead.

The last part of the import licensing rationale—the creation of incentives for investment—also leads to barriers to entry. The misallocation effects of these incentives have generally been recognized.[15] In addition, when favorable exchange rates (and rapid depreciation tax policies and low interest loans) encourage capital-intensive rather than labor-intensive production processes, the

[15] See Little, Scitovsky, and Scott, op.cit.

apparent economies of scale of the processes may be higher. There are higher levels of fixed costs that require larger volumes of output for amortization. My argument here is that production functions may be non-homogeneous and that the labor-intensive methods of production may not exhibit significant economies of scale while the capital-intensive methods do, because of the lumpiness of the capital equipment. Faced by some factor prices, entrepreneurs will choose labor-intensive methods and many producers can be in the market. Faced by different factor prices, entrepreneurs will choose capital-intensive methods, economies of scale will be important, and only a few producers can be in the market. One frequently observes both phenomena side by side in LDC's. Many industries are composed of hundreds or thousands of small labor-intensive cottage or workshop operations, the owners of which face expensive capital and cheap (family) labor, and a small handful of large capital intensive factories, the owners of which face much cheaper capital and comparatively expensive labor.

The high apparent economies of scale act as a barrier to entry in two ways. First, a government may be reluctant to grant licenses for the creation of new capacity in an industry if it appears that current production is not fully exhausting apparent economies of scale. The government may be sympathetic to pleas by the industry's current occupants that "there clearly is not any room for any new entrants." Second, potential entrants (beyond the cottage industry stage) may feel the same way. Even if there are no licenses hindering a potential entrant but there are cheap capital goods (created, say, by low tariffs), he will find the large-volume, capital-intensive method to be the cheapest, lowest-cost method. Under those circumstances, there indeed will be no room for him to enter as a large-scale producer. The general imperfection of capital markets in LDC's adds the absolute capital barrier to the picture. Potential entrants into an industry may not be able to obtain adequate financing for their venture and consequently cease to be an active threat to the industry's occupants. The ownership of banks and insurance companies by groups already involved in industry may well raise this barrier even higher.

Finally, the supply of entrepreneurial talent in LDC's may be a scarce factor and operate as a barrier to entry. Nepotistic practices by firms or family groupings will continue to keep these barriers high. Entrepreneurship may be a learning-by-doing process, in which a great deal of trial and error is necessary to develop the necessary skills and sort out the more skilled practitioners from the less skilled. To the extent that licenses and other barriers impede free entry, potential entrepreneurs may never get the opportunity. Papanek, though, has argued that all a government need do is provide the right incentives and the supply of entrepreneurs will come forth.[16] The right incentives are the promise of high profits. If this is true, LDC governments may face a difficult dilemma: To break the initial barrier of entrepreneurship, LDC's may have to create other (e.g., licensing) barriers. But if the newly developed entrepreneurial class uses its economic power to achieve significant political power, the artificially created barriers may never come down, and entrepreneurship may spread only slowly beyond the initial fortunate group.

[16] Gustav F. Papanek, "The Development of Entrepreneurship," *American Economic Review* (May 1962).

Monopoly—Dynamic Effects

The dynamic effects of monopolies are less well understood and less generally agreed upon than are the static effects. At dispute is the type of market structure that will best bring forth the inventions and innovations that offer increasing productivity and a superior range of products for an economy. It is generally accepted that at least a little bit of monopoly power is necessary to generate the margin necessary to finance the research on an invention or innovation, take the risks of introducing it, and enjoy the exploitation of it. The question is whether *more* than a little bit is necessary. Those who say no argue that competitive pressures are the best guarantee of rapid introduction and exploitation of innovations and that many important inventions have come from independent inventors or small businesses.[17] Those who say yes argue that important inventions can be financed only by the large research and development expenditures of large firms and that only large firms (with considerable market power) can afford the risks of innovation; rival pressure by corporate giants will be sufficient to bring forth the inventions and innovations.[18] Absolute size and relative market shares can easily get confused in this debate.[19]

It is not clear where the relevance of this argument lies for LDC's. Little is known about the capabilities of LDC companies to general inventions and innovations. Most

[17] See, for example, Walter Adams and Joel B. Dirlam, "Big Steel, Invention, and Innovation," *Quarterly Journal of Economics* (May 1966), and John Jewkes, David Sawyers, and Richard Stillerman, *The Sources of Invention*, 2nd edn. (New York, 1969).

[18] See, for example, John Kenneth Galbraith, *The New Industrial State* (Boston, 1967).

[19] For a review of the debate, see Scherer, *op.cit.*, Ch. 15.

large LDC companies are usually far smaller than the smallest company in the *Fortune* list of the 500 largest U.S. industrial companies or even the 200 largest non-American industrial companies. In 1969, only 7 of the largest 200 industrial companies outside the U.S. were based in LDC's. Of these, 5 were oil or mining companies and a sixth was government owned. The largest of these 7 would have ranked 116th in the United States by sales.[20] In Pakistan, the largest firm listed on the Karachi Stock Exchange in 1969 was the Karachi Electric Supply Co., with Rs.567.5 million in total assets. At the official exchange rate of Rs.4.76 = $1, this was equivalent to $119.2 million.[21] The largest manufacturing firm was Kohinoor Industries, a firm producing cotton textiles and industrial chemicals. It had total assets of Rs.313.9 million, equivalent to $65.9 million. This would have placed Kohinoor Industries at 727th on the list of the largest American industrial firms.[22]

Basic research in abstract fields is probably a luxury that most LDC's cannot presently afford. Rather, what is needed in the short run is research aimed at absorbing the new technology developed by industrial countries and adapting it to local conditions and to labor-intensive methods. This requires the modification of production processes, machine designs, and product designs, so as to encourage labor-intensive production methods.[23] What

[20] *Fortune* (May 1970), pp. 184-201 and (August 1970), pp. 142-146.

[21] Since most of the capital equipment for Pakistani companies was imported at the official exchange rate, evaluating a Pakistani company's assets in dollars at the official exchange rate is a reasonable procedure.

[22] *Fortune* (June 1970), pp. 100-116.

[23] For a historical perspective on the kind of adaptations that can take place, see Gustav Ranis, "Some Observations on the

absolute size and market structure in LDC's is best for this? There is no good evidence on this point. As noted earlier, large protected monopolies are likely to have a bias toward capital-intensive technologies and are unlikely to be interested in adapting their production methods in labor-intensive directions. The press of competition, then, from home or abroad, is probably an important ingredient in generating the proper research and adaptation.[24] But absolute size remains an open question. Clearly, cottage industry is unsuited to the role of technology adaptor. Beyond that, however, there is no presumption in favor of large or small. More evidence on the whole question of research and technological adaptation in LDC's—where, how, and why it is done—is badly needed.

Monopoly—Social and Political Effects

The social and political effects of monopoly are as important in LDC's as are the economic effects. Industrial monopoly profits mean a redistribution of income and the

---

Economic Framework for Optimum LDC Utilization of Technology," Center Discussion Paper No. 152, Yale University Economic Growth Center (August 1972). For a description of current adaptation, see Amir U. Khan and Bart Duff, "Development of Agricultural Mechanization Technologies at the International Rice Research Institute," Paper No. 72-02, Agricultural Engineering Department, International Rice Research Institute (January 1973).

[24] An alternative to relying on the structure of the private sector to provide the technology adaptations would be for the government to engage in the necessary research and development and to disseminate the information. This is the route that has generally been followed in agriculture. But the press of competition would still be necessary to ensure that the disseminated information was used.

generation of large wealth accumulations. This income and wealth, in turn, provide the base for political and social power for its owners. In a society in which the centers and sources of power are not widely diffused, the monopoly-generated power may attain significant levels. To some extent, it may simply serve as an offset or countervailing force to the traditional sources of power based on agriculture. But if the holders of industrial-based power come to be dominant or work out an acceptable compromise with the rural-based forces, this social and political power will be used to support and reinforce the monopoly-economic power. It becomes politically impossible, or at least extremely difficult, to remove the tariffs or import quotas or stop the price-fixing that is the source of the monopoly power. The ability of firms to gain economic advantage for themselves through the political process becomes related to their size and market power.[25] A request for tariffs, quotas, or licenses will be far more persuasive to a tariff commission or a legislature if it comes from one or a few industrialists representing large, powerful firms than if it comes from a group of small entrepreneurs.[26] The web of economic and political power becomes self-reinforcing.

[25] This is generally true for developed countries, in which independent sources of power are diffused and can be countervailing. It is likely to be yet more valid for developing countries, in which well-organized countervailing power centers are few. For some of the recent sociological studies of the reinforcing links among economic, political, and social power in the United States, see C. Wright Mills, *The Power Elite* (New York, 1956); G. William Domhoff, *Who Rules America?* (Englewood Cliffs, 1967); G. William Domhoff, *The Higher Circles* (Random House, 1970); and, at a more popular level, Morton Mintz and Jerry S. Cohen, *America, Inc.* (New York, 1971).

[26] See Fulda and Till, *op.cit.*, and Diaz-Alejandro, *op.cit.*, for

Perhaps the divergent interests of the industrial monopolists might be enough to provide countervailing power. After all, high tariffs and protection to the steel industry do mean higher costs to the industrial users of steel, and these users might use their influence to try to offset the steel industry's demands for protection. But there is no guarantee that this will occur. An industrial oligarchy might well find more on which it can agree than disagree, and conflicts are resolved at the expense of the rest of society. A system of cascaded tariffs—high tariffs to protect the steel industry and yet higher tariffs to protect steel users—may prove to be the easiest way to resolve potential conflicts.

Further, the effort by an LDC to mobilize its public resources for growth and development may be seriously retarded by the presence of a rich and powerful elite. Development inevitably requires the provision of large amounts of social overhead capital, the funds for which generally have to be raised through public taxation. The immediate personal costs of this taxation are usually clear and obvious; the benefits from the social overhead capital are usually more vague and diffuse and may well have some income redistributive aspects. If the rich elite provide an example to which the urban middle class aspires (and if, further, there is a general feeling that the elite attained and are maintaining their position through government favors or tax evasion, legal or illegal), the middle class may resist all taxation that limits their incomes, especially all direct taxation. The general spirit of a mobilization effort to attain growth and development will fail to develop.

---

evidence for India and Colombia on this point. The evidence from Pakistan is provided in Chapter 7, below.

In the case of oligopoly, wealth and its consequent power may be diffused in a few more hands than in the case of monopoly; but, since the industry members have similar interests and a strong incentive not to fall out over basic issues, the fundamental political outcome in LDC's may not be significantly different.

A second non-economic aspect of a protected monopoly is the apparent scope for arbitrary, non-maximizing activity on the part of the monopolist. Eccentric behavior by one competitor among many has no significant effect on overall market performance. Eccentric behavior by a monopolist will affect an entire market.

Monopoly, Profits, and Growth

A country's real income is decreased by the static allocative effects of a monopoly. Since saving is usually a function of real income, and saving, investment, and income growth are usually linked, growth may be reduced by the existence of monopoly. These effects will usually be swamped, however, by the direct income distribution effects on saving. By reducing his output and raising his price, the monopolist effects an income transfer away from consumers and to himself. If he has a different marginal propensity to save than do his consumers, overall saving will be affected. In the extreme, if the entire industrial sector were composed of monopolies in each market, there would be an overall redistribution of income away from purchasers of industrial products (the services and agriculture sectors) to the industrial sector. The extent to which this income transfer would be shared between industrial wage earners and industrial capitalists in a LDC would be determined by the balance between the pressures of unemployment and pressures by trade unions, government social welfare, and industrial paternalism. To the extent that a LDC government has both growth and a particular income distribution as its goals, the income distribution effect of a monopoly will be important for its own sake.

The issues of growth, monopoly profits, and income distribution warrant further treatment. Much of the discussion concerning LDC's has been concerned with growth and actions that will speed or hinder it. Until recently, few discussants have stopped to ask, "Growth for whom?" Yet one can use a simple Lewis surplus labor model to determine that the major income beneficiaries of growth—until the surplus labor in the economy is exhausted—will be the group that currently receives the major share of manufacturing value-added.[27] In many LDC's, this group is the industrialists.

This can be demonstrated fairly simply. The Lewis model assumes that marginal productivity is very low or zero in argriculture and that workers in argriculture receive income equal to their average product, which is close to subsistence. Wages in the industrial sector need only be higher than this by the margin necessary to attract workers from the countryside, though labor union and/or government social welfare efforts may keep industrial wages above this minimum. In any event, there is a large actual and potential supply of labor from the labor-surplus countryside that is willing to work in the industrial sector at the going wages. This press of surplus labor will keep industrial wages low (except for union or government efforts) until the surplus labor has been exhausted through the expansion of the industrial sector, this in turn

[27] W. Arthur Lewis, "Economic Development with Unlimited Supply of Labour," *The Manchester School* (May 1954).

being due to the reinvestment of the profits of the industrial sector.[28]

Until the surplus labor is exhausted, each additional unit of capital in the industrial sector will be able to be combined with labor being paid the same subsistence (or union) wage. We are thus in a world of fixed proportions, in which the marginal unit of capital will earn what the previous units of capital have earned, just as the marginal unit of labor will earn what the previous units have earned.[29] The 1967-1968 West Pakistan Census of Manufacturing Industries indicated that only 26.4% of value added in manufacturing (excluding sales and excise taxes) accrued to labor; the remaining 73.6% accrued to capital (to cover depreciation, taxes, interest, and profits).[30]

Growth along this pattern would mean an expansion in manufacturing employment—and a large rise in gross profits. If income distribution is measured according to capital and labor shares of the industrial product, the distribution will remain the same. But if income distribution is measured among individuals, and the number of profit receivers remains relatively constant, this pattern of growth will generate a sharp worsening of the income dis-

[28] Also, the rising average productivity in agriculture as workers leave will also tend to push wages up. But population growth in the countryside will dampen this tendency.

[29] Only if industrial prices fall will this pattern change. But if some of the minimum consumption of the workers is also industrial goods, wages will fall too, though not by as much.

[30] Government of Punjab, *Census of Manufacturing Industries of West Pakistan*, 1967-1968, mimeo (Lahore, 1970). Labor's share of manufacturing value added appears to have declined over time. In 1959-1960 labor's share was 47.9%; in 1954 it was 44.5%.

tribution. Further, this will continue to get worse until
the manufacturing sector becomes large enough to absorb all surplus labor and the industrialists have to start
bidding up the price of labor. How soon this occurs will
clearly depend on the size of the initial labor surplus, the
rate and bias of technological change in agriculture and
manufacturing, the rate of saving and investment by the
industrial sector, and the labor-intensiveness of the technology in the manufacturing sector. It could take a long
time, particularly if the rate of population growth is rapid
and if the incentives in the system are encouraging the
use of a capital-intensive technology.

This growth-profits-income-distribution nexus poses a
severe dilemma for LDC governments. High private
profits will mean either high consumption by the rich or
reinvestment, growth, but yet more high profits and a
substantial and growing wealth and power position for
the rich. Raising workers' wages through minimum wage
legislation, social welfare, and trade unions may siphon
off some of the profits, but it will make labor more expensive, discourage the use of labor-intensive techniques,
and thus reduce industrial employment. Further, in the
absence of effective taxing or saving of workers' incomes,
the reduced profits will slow down future capital accumulation and delay the eventual exhaustion of the labor
surplus. Only if governments can efficiently tax and re-
invest the profits will growth and equitable income distribution goals be simultaneously reached.

Concentration of Economic Power

Concentration of industrial economic power also has
economic and non-economic aspects. The economic aspects focus on multi-company ownership. In a number of
ways, these problems mirror the problems that have been

discussed in connection with the recent conglomerate merger boom in the United States.[31]

The possible advantages of multi-company ownership are its superior income-savings-investment capabilities in the face of imperfect capital markets, its risk-pooling advantages, and its ability to take advantage of economies of scale of management. All three arguments would seem to be especially relevant to LDC's, where capital markets are more imperfect, investment risks greater, and managerial talent in shorter relative supply than in developed countries.

The economic problems associated with multi-company ownership center on the possible stifling of existing or potential competition. In principle a multi-company owner has a "deep pocket"; he can use the income flows from other areas to subsidize the temporary losses of one part of his operation. This may allow him to drive out or discourage the entry of competitors who are less well financed and thus permit him to develop or strengthen his monopoly power in particular markets. This will be profitable, of course, only if the barriers to new entry are high. Reciprocal dealing arrangements, whereby a multi-company organization arranges favorable selling terms for one of its companies' products with an outside firm because other of its companies are important buyers of that outside firm's products, may restrict competition and raise the barriers to entry. Again, to the extent that entrepreneurial talent is scarce and capital markets imperfect, this discouragement to actual or potential competitors should be particularly relevant to LDC's.

---

[31] For a discussion of these problems in the United States, see U.S. Senate, Committee on the Judiciary, Subcommittee on Antitrust and Monopoly, *Economic Concentration*, Hearings, Part 8 (Washington, D.C., 1970).

Nepotistic practices by family-owned multi-company organizations may limit the growth and development of managerial talent in the LDC's. By favoring family members over outsiders, these organizations may effectively limit the potential new competition that they would have to face if the outsiders, after gaining experience, left the organization to start their own companies. This kind of favoritism could continue only if the individual companies had monopoly-oligopoly power or had deep pockets. Otherwise, the pressures of competition would force companies to hire the most talented personnel, regardless of family origin.

Also, the sheer size of multi-company organizations will often promote them to favored positions in the receipt of government contracts, import licenses, or investment licenses. They are thus able to perpetuate and strengthen their market positions and shut out new competitors.

Frequently, multi-company organizations in LDC's own or effectively control banks and insurance companies. As a consequence these banks and insurance companies are no longer likely to be neutral financiers, looking only for the highest rate of return. They are likely to favor the "in-house" industrial companies and, again, the multi-company organizations will have a strong advantage over potential new competitors.

The non-economic impact of concentration in the large is much the same as that discussed for simple monopoly, only more so. Even if each company within a multi-company organization is earning only a normal competitive return on capital, the sum of a number of normal returns may still amount to a significant income flow. If some of these companies possess monopoly power, the flow will be larger, and the likelihood of abuses increases. With significant concentration of industrial economic power, the political power flowing from economic power is concentrated in yet fewer hands; the possibility of internal conflicts of interest among entrepreneurs is further reduced. The general tone and nature of a country's economic, social, and political activity may be very different when a comparative handful of organizations or families controls a high percentage of a country's industrial assets than when this control is widely diffused.

Summary

The allocative and distributive effects of industrial concentration can be serious for LDC's. Many of the barriers to entry, which allow the consequences of industrial concentration to continue, have not been natural but have been created, whether deliberately or inadvertently, by LDC government policies. The non-economic effects, particularly the generation of political power that is used to reinforce economic power, are equally serious. Multi-company organizations, which are likely to be the basis of the concentration of economic power, have conflicting effects. They are a means of circumventing the barriers to entry that poorly developed capital markets create. But, in turn, they are likely to create other, and perhaps higher, barriers in their wake that will confront new entrepreneurs who try to follow. In the short run, some individual markets may function more efficiently. In the long run, the industrial sector may become concentrated in the hands of a comparatively small oligarchy, with serious consequences for the long-run social, political, and economic development of the country.

Chapter 3

The Pakistani Background

THE story of the growth of Pakistani industry has been told elsewhere, and only the major features need be repeated here.[1] At Partition in 1947, both wings of the newly created Pakistan were largely agricultural, with virtually no industry or attendant services. West Pakistani agriculture was based on cotton and wheat; East Pakistani agriculture centered on rice and jute. The collapse of the Korean War raw materials boom turned the terms of trade against Pakistani raw materials and in favor of manufactures. The refusal of Pakistan to devalue after the collapse of the raw materials boom meant that the demand for foreign exchange exceeded the supply. The eventual devaluation in 1955 did not really close the foreign exchange gap. Tariffs, foreign exchange licensing, and import quotas bridged the gap, and large incentives for the domestic production of manufactured goods were created. These were reinforced with tax advantages that yet further encouraged domestic production of manufactures.

A class of Pakistani industrialists developed in re-

[1] See Gustav F. Papanek, *Pakistani Development: Social Goals and Private Incentives* (Cambridge, Mass., 1967); Stephen R. Lewis, Jr., *Economic Policy and Industrial Growth in Pakistan* (London, 1969); and Stephen R. Lewis, Jr., *Pakistan: Industrialization and Trade Policies* (London, 1970).

sponse to these incentives.[2] Most had come from trading families, and many had migrated from India to Pakistan after Partition. Few had previously been in manufacturing. Nevertheless, they were able to respond robustly to the incentives, and the growth of manufacturing in Pakistan became one of the success stories of the LDC's. The national income figures indicate that, in real terms (1959-1960 prices), the value added in large-scale manufacturing grew eleven-fold between 1949-1950 and 1967-1968.[3] Measured at current prices, the percentage of GNP attributable to large-scale manufacturing grew from 1.7% in the first year to 8.2% in the last. Even more impressive was the continued growth of industry after a substantial base had been established. Between 1959-1960 and 1967-1968, the national income figures indicate that large-scale manufacturing grew in real terms by 172%, or 13% per year.

Industrial growth was initially based on cotton textiles in West Pakistan. High tariffs and quotas on imported textiles, combined with export taxes on the major domestic input, raw cotton, provided the major incentives. Industrial growth gradually spread to other textiles, food, beverages, tobacco, and other consumer goods. Manufactured exports received an extra stimulus in 1959 when

[2] For further background on the Pakistani industrialists, see Papanek, op.cit., Chapter II; Gustav F. Papanek, "The Industrial Entrepreneurs—Education, Occupational Background and Finance," in Development Policy: The Pakistan Experience, W. P. Falcon and G. F. Papanek, eds. (Cambridge, Massachusetts, 1971); and Hannah Papanek, "Pakistan's Big Businessmen: Muslim Separation, Entrepreneurship, and Partial Modernization," Economic Development and Cultural Change (October 1972).

[3] See Government of Pakistan, Ministry of Finance, Economic Survey 1970-71 (Islamabad, 1971), statistical section, pp. 2-5.

a bonus voucher system (see Chapter VI) provided some compensation for the overvalued exchange rate. The structure of incentives discouraged the production of capital goods and intermediates. As Table 3-1 indicates, in 1967-1968 at least 71.6% of the labor employed in large-scale manufacturing and 64.6% of the value added came from consumer goods industries.

TABLE 3-1

Employment and Value Added in West Pakistan
Consumer Goods Industries, 1967-1968

	Employment	Value Added (Excluding Indirect Taxes) (000)
Food	35,525	332,801
Beverage	1,325	14,583
Tobacco	8,114	132,634
Cotton textiles and ginning	160,731	678,505
Other textiles (except jute)	32,223	150,898
Footwear and apparel	7,186	34,266
Wood, cork, and allied products	1,128	4,150
Furniture	1,572	6,857
Paper products	1,740	12,710
Printing and publishing	7,799	59,034
Leather products	145	377
Pharmaceuticals	7,181	156,102
Cosmetics	688	7,854
Soap	2,019	17,579
Service and household machines	742	3,193
Electric fans	2,977	14,355
Electric lamps	549	42,738
Cycles	4,834	18,828
Misc.	8,524	45,871
Total	285,002	1,733,335
All manufacturing	398,226	2,684,848
Consumer goods as a %	71.6%	64.6%

SOURCE: Government of Punjab, *Census of Manufacturing Industries of West Pakistan*, 1967-1968, mimeo (Lahore, 1970).

Though the percentage rate of growth of manufacturing in East Pakistan was faster than in West Pakistan, East Pakistan started from a much lower base.[4] The difference in growth rates was never large enough to make up the absolute differences, and in 1967-1968 East Pakistan, with a population that was at least a fifth larger than that of West Pakistan, had a manufacturing sector that was only two-fifths the size of West Pakistan's, as measured by value added.

East Pakistan's industrial growth was initially based on manufactured jute textiles. There was no natural internal market for jute textiles comparable to the internal market for cotton textiles in West Pakistan. Virtually all jute manufactures were for export. Jute manufacturers received an implicit subsidy from the export tax on raw jute, which kept the domestic price of raw jute low. This was comparable to the effect of the export tax on raw cotton in West Pakistan. But West Pakistan cotton textiles received an extra subsidy from high protection levels that East Pakistan jute textiles, exported at the official rate of exchange, did not receive. Even after the export bonus voucher system was established in 1959 to aid exports, jute textile exports received less of an incentive than did cotton textile exports.[5] The Pakistani political system was not prepared to subsidize jute textiles to the same extent that it subsidized cotton textiles. Another indication of this was Pakistan's refusal to devalue in 1949

[4] Lewis, *Pakistan: Industrialization and Trade Policies*, p. 139.

[5] Jute textiles were given stamped bonus vouchers that were good only for importing jute textile machinery and materials and that, because of their limited use, were worth less than regular bonus vouchers. The stamped bonus vouchers were abolished only in 1967, and jute textile exports then received normal bonus vouchers.

following the devaluation of the British pound and the
Indian rupee. The justification at the time was that this
refusal gained Pakistan a terms-of-trade advantage in its
trade with India and that it allowed Pakistan to exploit
its world monopoly position in raw jute. Besides souring
Pakistani-Indian relations, however, this refusal made
jute over-priced, encouraged the growth of a jute industry
in India and the development of synthetic substitutes
abroad, and somewhat dulled the incentives for exporting
jute textiles.

Further, the actual and potential industrialists who
migrated to Pakistan mostly chose Karachi as their base
and preferred to establish their industrial operations in
West Pakistan. Along with the reduced economic incentives, the locational preference reduced the Pakistani
entrepreneurs' interest in jute textiles and in manufacturing in East Pakistan generally.

As a consequence, jute textiles never provided the same
size industrial base as did cotton textiles in West Pakistan. Though jute textiles grew rapidly after 1953, the
initial base was much smaller, and in 1967-1968 jute
textiles in East Pakistan represented only two-fifths of
the value added and the same fraction of the value of
production of cotton textiles in West Pakistan. Also,
relatively more of the industrial activity in the east was
undertaken by a government agency, the East Pakistan
Industrial Development Corporation. Finally, the industrial growth that followed jute displayed a pattern similar
to that of West Pakistan: food and beverages, tobacco,
textiles and other consumer goods.

Though the overall rate of industrial growth in Pakistan was high, the opportunity costs of that growth were
also high. Lewis and Guisinger found that most of the
industrial sectors in Pakistan were receiving large sub-

sidies to their value added through the tariff and licensing system, even if measured with a hypothetically devalued exchange rate.[6] A number of industries were being supported solely by the explicit and implicit subsidies; in the absence of this protection, they would have generated negative value added and would have ceased to exist. Similarly, Hufbauer found that the export incentive system was generating large subsidies to value added.[7] Thus, besides the high profits that were generated by these schemes, resources were being allocated inefficiently. Unless one were willing to value all of the inputs into industry at a zero opportunity cost, one would have to conclude that the real welfare gains would have been higher if the rate of industrial growth had been slower. The inputs that actually entered manufacturing had been allocated away from sectors where their value to overall Pakistani income would have been higher.[8]

Further, the rapid rate of industrial growth was not matched by as rapid a rate of employment growth. Though value added in large-scale manufacturing grew in real terms by 172% between 1959-1960 and 1967-

[6] Stephen R. Lewis, Jr., and Stephen E. Guisinger, "Measuring Protection in a Developing Country: The Case of Pakistan," *Journal of Political Economy* (December 1968).

[7] Gary C. Hufbauer, "West Pakistan Exports: Effective Taxation, Policy Promotion, and Sectoral Discrimination," in *Development Policy: The Pakistan Experience*, W. P. Falcon and G. F. Papanek, eds. (Cambridge, Massachusetts, 1971).

[8] Another way of expressing this point is found in Little, Scitovsky, and Scott, *Industry and Trade in Some Developing Countries*, pp. 73-75. When industrial value added was recalculated at world prices, the contribution of large-scale industry in Pakistan to gross domestic expenditure in 1963-1964 dropped from 7.0% to 0.4%. The contribution of large-scale manufacturing to overall GDP growth between 1950-1952 and 1964-1966 became negligible.

1968, employment grew by only 41%.[9] Though the latter rate, equivalent to 4.3% per year, was somewhat faster than the rate of population growth, it was far too low to make a serious dent in the unemployment and underemployment problem that Pakistan faced.[10]

The high level of profits and the realization that a comparatively small group of industrialists were undertaking most of the industrial activity—and that some of these same industrialists controlled most of the banking system and the insurance industry—began to cause concern. The First Five-Year Plan (1955-1960) and the Second Five-Year Plan (1960-1965) were silent on the subject of ownership concentration. But a Credit Inquiry Commission in 1959 found that 60% of all bank credit went to only 222 accounts. A Cartel Study Group was formed in 1963 and issued a report, but the report was never released. Professor Louis Loss from the Harvard Law School wrote a report in 1964 that urged that the Karachi Stock Market be regulated along the lines of the United States securities markets, so that more investors would enter the market and ownership would become more diversified. Meanwhile, in the budget of July 1963, the government proposed an extra tax on corporations that had gone public by listing their shares on the Karachi Stock Exchange but that still had over 50% of their shares in fewer than 20 hands. Since this was true of 89 of the 119 non-government-controlled listed companies,

[9] The employment figures are from the Censuses of Manufacturing Industries for the two years.

[10] For a critique of the overall inability of the Pakistan economy to meet the challenge of labor absorption, see Keith B. Griffen and Bruce Glassburner, "An Evaluation of Pakistan's Third Five Year Plan," *Journal of Development Studies* (July 1966), pp. 452-454.

the stock market took a dive. The government promptly suspended the proposal but kept it hanging over the stock market until 1968. In that year the government issued a "grandfather" exclusion to all firms already listed but insisted that all newly listed firms must offer over 50% of their shares to the public or face the tax.

President Ayub Khan, in his foreword to the Third Five-Year Plan (1965-1970), declared: "It will be our firm policy, therefore, to prevent excessive concentration of income and wealth in the hands of a few. . . ."[11] The rest of the plan, though, was silent on the concentration issue, except for a declaration that the dis-investment of government-controlled industries should be done by converting them into public companies with a large number of shareholders.[12] Three years later Mahbub ul Haq, the Chief Economist for the Planning Commission, attracted great notice when he told a management seminar in Karachi in April 1968 that economic power in Pakistan was concentrated in the hands of 20 families.[13] In 1969, in the aftermath of the unrest that brought down the Ayub Khan government, Pakistan's first Monopoly Control Ordinance was drafted and issued for comment, and in 1970 the Ordinance was put into law. The Fourth Five-Year Plan (1970-1975) devoted a considerable amount of space to the problem of industrial concentration, overall ownership and control concentration, and the consequent maldistribution of income and wealth. "In the past, the [development] strategy was based essentially on the premise that capital is shy and that enterprise needs to be brought up with the help of special incentives in the

[11] Government of Pakistan, Planning Commission, *Third Five-Year Plan, 1965-70* (Karachi, 1965), p. v.

[12] *Ibid.*, p. 108.

[13] *Business Recorder* (Karachi), April 25, 1968, p. 1.

form of subsidies, protection, and tax concessions. . . . However, the cost of development under this strategy for the private sector continued to rise. The cost is to be measured in terms of the maldistribution of income in the economy, concentration of ownership and economic power, and growing social tensions."[14]

[14] Government of Pakistan, Planning Commission, *Fourth Five-Year Plan, 1970-75* (Karachi, 1970), p. 81.

Chapter 4

Concentration of Industrial Economic Power

MUCH attention has been given in Pakistan to the question of how much of the industrial sector is controlled by the leading industrial families. Unfortunately, casual empiricism tended to dominate the discussion in the late 1960's, and there was little in the way of verifiable and meaningful analysis. It is possible, however, to put together in a systematic manner a reasonably complete picture of the holdings of the industrial families and relate it to a meaningful total for the entire manufacturing sector. That is the task of this chapter.

The chapter proceeds as follows: After a review of the past estimates of overall concentration, we discuss the problems of measuring overall concentration and explain the measures, methods, and sources used. Next, we verify the proposition asserted in Chapter 1 that foreign firms are a comparatively unimportant factor in Pakistan's industrial sector. With these preliminaries completed, we turn to the task of measuring overall domestic concentration in 1968, the last "typical" year in the Pakistani economy before the country broke apart. This task requires a number of successive approximations, beginning with the "hard" figures of the Karachi Stock Exchange and ending with estimates of all manufacturing in Pakistan. Pakistani concentration figures are compared over time and with estimates made for other countries. Separate concentration figures are presented for banks and insurance companies. The chapter concludes with a discussion of interlocking directorates in Pakistan.

Past Estimates of Overall Concentration

Three prominent estimates of overall concentration have previously been made. Sobhan, writing in 1965, noted that in the 1959-1960 Census of Manufacturing Industries, "75 units or 2.1 per cent of the total receive 43.8 per cent of all value added. If, however, we remember that these 75 units are themselves owned directly or indirectly by a much smaller nucleus of families then we can visualize the degree of concentration of corporate wealth. What indications there are of recent developments in the exhilarating atmosphere for business created by the budgets of the last 5 years indicates this concentration has possibly become even more acute."[1]

Papanek, writing in 1967, found that, "While there were over 3,000 individual firms in Pakistan in 1959, only 7 individuals, families or foreign corporations controlled one-quarter of all private industrial assets and one fifth of all industrial assets. Twenty-four units controlled nearly half of all private industrial assets. . . . It is also reported that approximately 15 families owned about three-quarters of all the shares in banks and insurance companies."[2] Mahbub ul Haq in 1968 claimed that the 20 largest families controlled 66% of the total industrial effort of the country, 70% of the total insurance funds, and 80% of the total bank assets.[3]

---

[1] Rehman Sobhan, "Strategy for Industrialization in Pakistan" in *Third Five-Year Plan and Other Papers*, Anwar Iqbal Qureshi, ed. (Rawalpindi, 1965), p. 109.

[2] Gustav F. Papanek, *Pakistan's Development: Social Goals and Private Incentives*, pp. 67-68.

[3] *Business Recorder* (Karachi), April 25, 1968, p. 1.

Haq's 20 families were expanded in most of the following discussions to 22, and the overall concentration problem has become known as the problem of "the 22 families." Unfortunately, Haq did not reveal the basis of his claim, and there appears to have been no careful study of the question since Papanek's survey of 1959 conditions. At the time of the discussion and enactment of the Pakistani Monopoly Control Ordinance in 1969 and 1970, there were no hard data to shape the public discussion and, to my knowledge, none since then.[4]

Measuring Overall Concentration

One could choose to measure overall concentration on the basis of ownership (or wealth) or on the basis of control. The difference between the two arises because some minority stockholders of a company exercise no effective control over the operations and policies of a company, and other stockholders, owning less than 100% of the shares (and, frequently far less than 50%), effectively control companies.[5]

[4] One brief, ambitious attempt appeared in the *Pakistan Times* on October 6, 7, and 8, 1969. Twenty-six of the 43 groups included in this study were included in that study. But the author restricted himself to an analysis of firms on the Karachi Stock Exchange, he used paid up capital as his measure of assets, he made a number of errors in attributing companies to controlling families, and many of the issues were not clearly delineated. Obviously, the journalistic factors of time and space were important constraints on the articles. See "Monopolies in Pakistan," installments I, II, and III, by "Economist," in the *Pakistan Times*, October 6, 1969, p. 6; October 7, 1969, p. 6; and October 8, 1969, p. 6.

[5] The classic study in this field is Adolf Berle and Gardiner Means, *The Modern Corporation and Private Property* (New York, 1932). See also P. Sargant Florence, *Ownership, Control,*

Control has been chosen as the basis for measurement in this study for two reasons. First, it represents the economic and political power that might be wielded by the entrepreneurs under discussion. It is comparatively unimportant whether an entrepreneur owns 40% of a firm or 90% of a firm; if he effectively controls it, then it represents potential power at his command.[6] Second, control is easier to determine than ownership and wealth. One can only guess what percentage of the shares of a family-controlled company, Adamjee Industries, Ltd., is owned by the Adamjee family. The family's total wealth is based on real estate and trading interests, as well as industrial holdings, and these would require even less precise guesses. But there is little doubt that the Adamjee family effectively controls Adamjee Industries. The overall wealth and income figures for the large families would indeed be interesting, especially for income distribution analyses, but the data are unavailable.[7] For now, control —and the power attendant to it—will have to suffice.

The best measure of industrial economic power across

---

and Success of Large Companies (London, 1961). For a recent survey of the American ownership-control situation in large American corporations, see Robert J. Larner, "Ownership and Control in the 200 Largest Non-Financial Corporations, 1929 and 1963," *American Economic Review* (September 1966). For the problems generated by the divorce of ownership from control see Edward S. Mason, ed., *The Corporation and Modern Society* (Cambridge, Mass., 1959).

[6] This is especially true if the commercial laws afford little protection to minority stockholders, as was true for Pakistan.

[7] In Chapter 7, I make some very rough and incomplete guesses at income figures, based only on the industrial holdings of these families.

the economy would be based on the value added generated by the firms under discussion, since there would be relatively few measurement problems. Unfortunately, value added is simply not available by individual firms, and this approach has to be discarded. Similarly, employment by individual firms is not available, so a measure based on employment cannot be used.

Production and sales figures are available for firms and for all manufacturing, but these present severe hazards because of the problems of vertical integration. Suppose a family owned a separate cotton spinning plant and a weaving plant, and it listed separately the sales of yarn from the spinning plant to the weaving plant and the sale of woven cloth. This family would appear to be almost twice as important as the family that owned an integrated spinning-weaving factory and only sold cloth. For this reason, sales are an unsatisfactory measure.

I have chosen book value of total assets of the controlled firms for my measure of control. There are problems of asset evaluation. The same type of imported capital equipment may have different rupee costs, depending on its origin, whether it was bought with tied aid funds, and what tariff or bonus voucher rate was paid. Also, depreciation accounting would affect the book value of assets. Rapid depreciation would mean that book value was understated; the absence of depreciation (because of tax holidays) would mean that book value was overstated. Still, despite its drawbacks, total assets seems to be the best available measure, and certainly superior to sales. I have chosen total assets rather than net worth (total assets less debt obligations) because the latter is more appropriate to wealth, whereas the former gets closer to the economic power and control concept that

I am seeking. One must, as a consequence, avoid counting all industrial assets, including debt obligations, and also counting bank and insurance company assets, most of which are the debt obligations of the industrial firms. This would be double counting. Thus, I have provided separate measures of the control of banks and insurance companies.

Some clarification of the accounting concept of total assets may be needed. Total assets of a company, through the rules of double-entry accounting, are definitionally equal to total liabilities. They can be computed by adding the fixed assets less depreciation and the current assets (cash and securities, inventories, and accounts receivable) of a firm or by summing the invested capital, the reinvested earnings or "surplus," long-term fixed liabilities (e.g., bonds), and short-term fixed liabilities (e.g., short-term bank loans). These totals represent the total size of the firm, at least as far as accounting rules will permit.

Some analysts of the Pakistani corporation data have used a different measure: "total capital employed," which is the sum of invested capital, surplus, and long-term fixed liabilities.[8] This measure neglects short-term liabilities. I believe that this measure is a poorer one to use, since it understates the full size of companies. Further, until 1970 the floating of long-term debt was discouraged by the tax and banking laws, and many firms had to rely

[8] See Khadija Haq and Moin Baqai, "Savings and Financial Flows in the Corporate Sector, 1959-63," *Pakistan Development Review* (Autumn 1967); and Shahid Amjad Chaudhry, "Private Foreign Investment in Pakistan," *Pakistan Development Review* (Spring 1970). The State Bank of Pakistan compilations of the corporate balance sheets have a separate line for "total capital employed," which encourages this practice.

on short-term debt, which was constantly renewed and rolled over, to provide long-term finance for themselves. Thus, even if one wanted a measure that included only effective long-term financing, it would be erroneous to exclude all short-term debt in Pakistan.

The Sample and Sources

As mentioned above, the problem of overall concentration in Pakistan has frequently been labeled the problem of "the 22 families." However, rather than limit my investigations to just 22 families, I expanded my research to include as many of the large, powerful families and groups[9] involved in manufacturing in Pakistan as possible. Data were available for 43 groups: 42 multi-company groupings and 1 large single-company complex. All but 4 of these organizations are identified with particular families. The remaining 4 are close associations of non-related businessmen who operate together. Since the prime focus of this study is on manufacturing, a few organizations that were important in trade or shipping but that had little or no manufacturing interests were excluded.

My sources of information have been company reports and lists of company chairmen and directors, the biographical data contained in "Who Is Who in Pakistani Business" compendia, and interviews with individuals close to Pakistani business circles. In only a few cases were there any questions as to who controlled a particular company, and I relied on the interview sources to settle most of these questions.

The State Bank of Pakistan compilation of the balance sheet figures of firms listed on the Karachi Stock Ex-

[9] The terms "families" and "groups" will be used interchangeably in this study.

change provided the primary source of information on the assets of firms controlled by the 43 important families and groups. It also provided a starting point for determining the total assets of all firms in manufacturing, against which the control of the 43 leading groups should be compared. The Karachi Exchange is relatively well developed by LDC standards. There was a tradition in pre-Partition India of large firms issuing publicly traded equity, and this carried over to modern India and Pakistan. Tax policy in Pakistan continued to encourage large firms to go public. In 1967-1968, the firms engaged in manufacturing that were listed on the Karachi Exchange accounted for just under 50% of the estimated assets of all manufacturing firms in Pakistan. Over 80% of total assets controlled by the 43 important families and groups included in this study were in companies listed on the Karachi Exchange. The figures are readily available, so no estimation or extrapolation is required. We have, then, a good, solid place to begin.

For a complete picture of overall concentration, however, we need to expand beyond the Karachi Exchange to an estimate of all manufacturing assets. This is done by successive approximations. First, the assets of firms listed on the Dacca Stock Exchange are estimated and included. Then the non-manufacturing firms are dropped from the sample. Finally, an estimate is made for the assets of all manufacturing firms, including unlisted firms.

The details on the basis for these estimates are contained in the appendix to this chapter. Briefly, estimates are required for the firms listed on the Dacca Stock Exchange because the State Bank of Pakistan did not compile balance sheets for these firms, and no yearbooks or other ready sources of information are available for these firms for 1968. For many firms, data for 1966 and 1967

were available, and these were expanded to a 1968 estimate. For others, knowledge of the physical characteristics
of the company (e.g., the number of spindles and looms
of a cotton textile factory) permitted estimation of its
assets. For the unlisted companies of the 43 families and
groups the total assets were estimated from information
concerning their physical characteristics or from estimates of net worth. The estimate for all Pakistani manufacturing assets starts with the value of fixed assets from
Censuses of Manufacturing Industries and expands these
figures, using information based on the assets and physical capacities of a number of important industries. Also,
estimates of foreign-controlled assets and government-
controlled assets in manufacturing are made.

We have, then, a progression from the solid figures of
the Karachi Stock Exchange through to estimates of the
assets of all manufacturing. At each stage in this progression, totals, shares, and concentration figures will be
provided.

Foreign Control

We can start first by substantiating the claim that was
made in the introductory chapter that foreign ownership
and control in Pakistan's manufacturing sector has been
comparatively small. Chaudhry argues that foreigners
owned 15%-17% of all corporate assets in Pakistan in
1967.[10] But he did not offer any estimate for manufacturing alone.

The easiest place to begin is the Karachi Stock Exchange. There were 197 non-financial companies listed
on the Karachi Stock Exchange in 1968, of which 171
were engaged in manufacturing. These companies had

[10] Chaudhry, op.cit.

total assets of Rs.7,293.4 million. There were 11 foreign-controlled companies listed on the Exchange.[11] These companies had total assets of Rs.887.7 million. Thus, foreign firms accounted for 12.2% of the manufacturing assets listed on the Karachi Exchange.[12]

These figures provide a preliminary estimate, but it is surely an overestimate of the foreign control of all manufacturing. Foreign firms tended to be larger than Pakistani firms and hence were more likely to be listed on the Karachi Exchange. We can, instead, use an estimate of the overall assets in manufacturing and an estimate for all foreign-controlled assets in manufacturing (the details of the latter are found in the appendix, part C). These estimates indicate that for 1968 foreign-controlled companies accounted for Rs.1,120.4 million out of Rs.15,059.0 million for all manufacturing firms, or 7.4%. This is probably closer to the true mark than the previous estimate of foreign control. This is, of course, an estimate subject to error, but even if the true foreign assets are 25% larger than the estimates, foreign control would still come to only 9.2%.

Some support for the general magnitude of this last estimate can be gained from the West Pakistan Census of Manufacturing Industries. The CMI showed foreign firms in 1967-1968 accounting for 3.4% of manufacturing employment and 4.7% of the value of production in West Pakistan. Joint enterprises accounted for another 5.8% of employment and 13.2% of output. The totals

[11] The basic source of this determination was the list of members of the Overseas Investors Chamber of Commerce and Industry.

[12] If the estimated assets for firms listed exclusively on the Dacca Stock Exchange were added to the base, this percentage would drop to 10.4%.

for the two categories are 8.2% of employment and 17.9% of production. But many of the joint enterprises were not controlled by foreigners, and the comparable percentages for East Pakistan, though unavailable, were surely lower, which would have decreased the averages for all Pakistan. The general magnitudes of the figures from the West Pakistan CMI, then, are in agreement with the estimate of 7.4% based on total assets.

The estimate is smaller than that given by Chaudhry because I have restricted the figures to manufacturing, focused on control rather than ownership, and used total assets rather than net worth or "total capital employed" as a base.

There is no absolute standard against which this estimate of foreign control can be judged. Rather, some rough-and-ready international comparisons can be made. Brandenburg has compiled lists of the 30 largest enterprises and their owners in 6 Latin American countries.[13] Unfortunately (for comparison purposes), Brandenburg includes banks, electric utilities, railroads, and mining and petroleum companies in his totals, so that his finding of an average foreign ownership among 30 top companies in the 6 countries of 16.4% is difficult to compare to my estimate for Pakistan. The exclusion of non-manufacturing enterprises from Brandenburg's sample (leaving 15-20 companies per country), would yield, I believe, a foreign ownership component of about 25% among the largest companies. This would range from roughly 40% in Argentina, Brazil, and Chile to 20% for Colombia, 10% for Mexico, and 0% for Venezuela. By comparison, of the 20 largest firms listed on the Karachi Stock

[13] Frank Brandenburg, *The Development of Latin American Private Enterprise* (Washington, D.C., 1964).

Exchange, 3 are foreign-controlled and these 3 account for 19% of the assets of the 20.

A recent study of the ownership and control of the 299 largest manufacturing companies in Australia found that foreigners had 36% of the total shareholders' funds and controlled firms that comprised 52% of the total assets of the 299-company sample.[14] The appropriate comparison would be with the Pakistan estimate of 12.2% based on the full Karachi Stock Exchange sample. In Canada, the percentage of all manufacturing controlled by foreigners in 1962 was estimated to be 60%.[15] The comparable Pakistani estimate is much lower.

Thus, it appears that foreign ownership and control of manufacturing assets in Pakistan is low by international comparison. Further there is only a small amount of mining activity in Pakistan (mining and quarrying accounted for only 0.3% of GNP in 1967-1968) and foreign firms are not heavily involved. It is not surprising, therefore, that foreign ownership has not been a political issue in Pakistan, whereas it has been an important one in Canada, Australia, Argentina, Brazil, and Chile.

One can ask, further, why foreign investment in Pakistan has been so low. The 1959 Statement of Industrial Policy promised foreign investors freedom to repatriate profits and capital, freedom from nationalization, and elimination of double taxation. The Pakistani government has repeatedly issued assurances that foreign investment would be welcome. One Pakistani magazine even went so far as to describe Pakistan as "a paradise" for

[14] E. L. Wheelwright and J. Miskelly, *Anatomy of Australian Manufacturing Industry* (Sydney, 1967), pp. 20, 55.

[15] A. E. Safarian, *Foreign Ownership of Canadian Industry* (Toronto, 1966), p. 14.

foreign investors.[16] Why, then, have foreign investors shied away?

First, foreigners have not been free to enter any industry that they chose. Foreign firms have generally been excluded from the lucrative consumer goods industries such as cotton and woolen textiles, sugar, and edible oils. A few British firms from pre-Partition days are in the tea and cigarette industries, but these are exceptions. A list distributed by the Pakistan government in 1969 concerning prospective investment indicated 41 industries in which "no foreign collaboration in any form is required."[17] These were mostly consumer goods, plus cement, bricks, steel, re-rolling, and cast-iron foundries. For an additional 43 industries, including cotton and woolen textiles, bicycles, razor blades, simple metal products like screws and wire, and some complex products like mining machinery and aircraft, "no foreign equity is needed but technological collaboration is needed." Finally, there were 37 industries in which "foreign investment is needed." Only pharmaceuticals, dairy products, and poultry products would qualify as consumer goods in this last list. The remainder were export industries, basic industrial chemicals, specialized metal and glass products, and high technology industries. Thus, the menu of investable industries for foreigners has been considerably less appetizing than that in other countries.

Second, some foreign firms seem to have been wary of becoming enmeshed in Pakistan's very complex foreign exchange system. Despite official policy welcoming

[16] "Pakistan—A Paradise for Investors," *Finance and Industry* (February 1969), pp. 33-34.

[17] This is an untitled list, dated July 27, 1969, distributed by the Department of Industrial Promotion and Supplies.

foreign investment, actual administration of the foreign exchange system raised the spectre of foreigners experiencing delays and difficulties in receiving import licenses and repatriating funds.

Third, Pakistan has thus far not been found to be rich in mineral resources, so the foreign investment that frequently dominates the extraction industries of LDC's has not been present. With the relative absence of foreign investment, Pakistan may have thereby foregone some real resources from the world at large, but it also escaped a political problem that has bedeviled many other countries.

Overall Concentration in Pakistan

We can now tackle directly the question of industrial economic power by Pakistani families and groupings. We again start with the firms listed on the Karachi Stock Exchange. There were 197 non-financial companies listed on the Karachi Stock Exchange in 1968.[18] These companies had total assets of Rs.9,726.0 million.[19] These figures include gas and electric utilities, transportation, construction, mining, storage, and trading firms, so they represent modern large-scale industry in a broader sense than just manufacturing. The 43 important families and groups controlled 98 listed non-financial companies with total assets of Rs.5,165.7 million, or 53.1% of the total

[18] Financial companies—banks and insurance companies—have been excluded to avoid the double counting of assets, as mentioned in the text.

[19] The compilation by the State Bank of Pakistan lists the 1968 total as Rs. 9,260.0 million. But the bank's compilation neglects a few firms that extended their accounting year beyond calendar 1968 and that therefore failed to issue a balance sheet in 1968. I have added the 1967 total assets of these few firms to the 1968 totals for the year.

assets for non-financial firms listed on the Exchange. Column (1) of Table 4-1 shows the listed assets controlled by each of the 43 important families and groups, along with the totals for the largest 4, 10, 20, 30, and all 43 groups. In Table 4-2, these totals are related to the total of all assets of non-financial companies listed on the Exchange. The 4 largest families controlled a fifth of the total assets of non-financial companies, the 10 largest families controlled over a third of the total assets, and the 30 largest controlled over half.

Table 4-2 also provides the totals on the Exchange for all privately controlled non-financial companies (i.e., government-controlled firms are excluded), all Pakistani-controlled firms (i.e., foreign-controlled firms are excluded), and private Pakistani-controlled firms (i.e., both government- and foreign-controlled firms are excluded), against which the control of the 43 groups can be measured. Of the private Pakistani-controlled firms, for example, the 4 leading families controlled over a quarter of the assets, the 10 leading families controlled just under half of the assets, and all 43 families and groups controlled just under three-quarters of the assets.

As a check on total assets as a measure of control, I also computed the percentages of net worth, fixed assets after depreciation, and sales accounted for by the 43 families and groups. These are compared to both the total values listed on the stock exchange and the total listed for domestic privately controlled firms in Table 4-3. The percentages of each measure are reasonably close to the figures for total assets. We seem to be measuring something that consistently appears, regardless of the measurement scale used.

To see if the asset concentration figures had changed much over time, I computed similar percentages for

TABLE 4-1

Control of Industrial and Manufacturing Assets in Pakistan, 1968 (Rs. million)

	All Non-Financial Assets Listed on the Karachi Stock Exchange (1)	All Non-Financial Assets Listed on the Karachi and Dacca Stock Exchanges (2)	All Manu-facturing Assets Listed on the Karachi and Dacca Stock Exchanges (3)	All Manu-facturing Assets, Listed and Unlisted (4)
1. Dawood	557.8	557.8	557.8	557.8
2. Saigol	529.8	529.8	528.9	556.5
3. Adamjee	437.6	450.9	450.9	473.2
4. Jalil (Amin)	418.8	418.8	418.8	418.8
5. Shaikh	325.4	325.4	318.5	342.7
6. Fancy	280.4	280.4	215.4	330.5
7. Valika	320.2	320.2	252.8	252.8
8. Bawany	237.4	237.4	237.4	237.4
9. Bashir (Crescent)	199.5	199.5	199.5	199.5
10. Wazir Ali	132.7	132.7	132.7	178.5
11. Ghandara	153.2	153.2	153.2	163.2
12. Ispahani	90.6	90.6	90.6	154.0
13. Habib	128.1	128.1	126.2	136.2
14. Khyber Textile Group	127.5	127.5	127.5	127.5
15. Nishat Group	64.6	64.6	64.6	126.9
16. BECO	113.6	113.6	113.6	113.6
17. Gul Ahmed	21.1	21.1	21.1	109.2
18. Arag (Haji Habib)	32.4	32.4	32.4	105.4
19. Hafiz	100.1	100.1	100.1	105.3
20. H. A. Karim	95.4	95.4	95.4	95.4
21. Millwala	–	–	–	95.0
22. Hyesons	68.4	68.4	68.4	94.3
23. Dada	48.0	48.0	48.0	90.6
24. Premier Group	77.3	77.3	77.3	89.3
25. Hussein Ebrahim	88.4	88.4	88.4	88.4
26. Monnoo	7.9	7.9	7.9	79.4
27. Maulabaksh	58.9	58.9	58.9	79.1
28. Adam	45.1	45.1	45.1	78.0
29. A. K. Khan	–	18.2	18.2	74.9
30. A. A. Ghani	41.2	41.2	41.2	71.2
31. Rangoonwala	44.5	44.5	44.5	68.2
32. Haroon	13.1	13.1	13.1	61.2

TABLE 4-1 (Continued)

	All Non-Financial Assets Listed on the Karachi Stock Exchange (1)	All Non-Financial Assets Listed on the Karachi and Dacca Stock Exchanges (2)	All Manufacturing Assets Listed on the Karachi and Dacca Stock Exchanges (3)	All Manufacturing Assets, Listed and Unlisted (4)
33. Hirjina	–	–	–	60.8
34. Shaffi	60.2	60.2	60.2	60.2
35. Fakir Chand	–	59.6	59.6	59.6
36. Haji Hashan	33.3	33.3	33.3	58.5
37. Dadabhoy	–	–	–	53.9
38. Shahnawaz	36.3	36.3	36.3	52.8
39. Fateh Textile Group	52.7	52.7	52.7	52.7
40. Noon	36.0	36.0	36.0	48.0
41. Hoti	40.6	40.6	40.6	45.8
42. Ghulam Faruque	36.7	36.7	36.7	36.7
43. Haji Dost Mohd.	20.4	20.4	20.4	31.6
Total, Largest 4[a]	1,944.0	1,957.3	1,956.4	2,006.3
" " 10[a]	3,450.1	3,473.4	3,333.0	3,547.7
" " 20[a]	4,472.2	4,495.3	4,354.0	4,884.4
" " 30[a]	4,962.7	5,010.7	4,868.6	5,624.6
Total, All 43	5,165.2	5,266.1	5,124.0	6,314.6

[a] Totals refer to largest 4, 10, etc. in that column.
SOURCE: See text.

firms listed on the Karachi Stock Exchange in 1962. Table 4-4 shows these figures. A comparison of 1962 with 1968 indicates that the share of the largest 4, 10, and 20 groups declined somewhat, but that the share of all 43 groups remained relatively unchanged. The largest groups had listed most of their companies on the Karachi Exchange before 1962. Though these companies grew rapidly (and some new companies were added), the growth of all assets on the exchange, buoyed considerably by the listing of new firms, outstripped them. But new

TABLE 4-2

Percentage Control of All Non-Financial Assets Listed on the
Karachi Stock Exchange, 1968 (Rs. million)

	All Assets	All Assets of Privately Controlled Firms[a]	All Assets of Pakistani-Controlled Firms[b]	All Assets of Private Pakistani-Controlled Firms[c]
	Rs.9,726.0	Rs.7,898.6	Rs.8,838.3	Rs.7,010.9
Largest 4 groups Rs.1,944.0	20.0%	24.6%	22.0%	27.7%
" 10 " 3,450.1	35.5	43.7	39.0	49.2
" 20 " 4,472.2	46.0	56.6	50.6	63.8
" 30 " 4,962.7	51.0	62.8	56.1	70.8
All 43 " 5,165.2	53.1	65.4	58.4	73.7

[a] Excludes government-controlled firms.
[b] Excludes foreign-controlled firms.
[c] Excludes government- and foreign-controlled firms.

SOURCES: Table 4-1; Appendix to Chapter IV.

TABLE 4-3

Comparative Measures of Control of All Non-Financial
Assets Listed on the Karachi Stock Exchange, 1968

	All Firms				All Private Pakistani-Controlled Firms			
	Total Assets	Net Worth	Fixed Assets After Depreciation	Sales	Total Assets	Net Worth	Fixed Assets After Depreciation	Sales
Largest 4 Groups	20.0%	18.1	17.4	21.6	27.7	24.6	24.8	29.5
Largest 10 Groups	35.5	34.7	31.9	37.3	49.2	47.1	45.5	51.0
Largest 20 Groups	46.0	46.6	42.5	47.8	63.8	63.3	60.6	65.3
Largest 30 Groups	51.0	52.2	48.2	52.2	70.8	70.8	68.7	71.3
All 43 Groups	53.1	54.7	50.7	53.5	73.7	74.2	72.2	73.1

SOURCES: Table 4-2; State Bank of Pakistan, *Balance Sheet Analysis of Joint Stock Companies Listed on the Karachi Stock Exchange, 1964-69* (Karachi, 1971).

TABLE 4-4

Percentage Control of All Non-Financial Assets Listed on the Karachi Stock Exchange, 1962 (Rs. million)

		All Assets	All Assets of Privately Controlled Firms	All Assets of Pakistani-Controlled Firms	All Assets of Private Pakistani-Controlled Firms
		Rs.3,090.0	Rs.2,636.1	Rs.2,726.9	Rs.2,273.0
Largest 4 groups Rs.	784.2	25.4%	29.7%	28.8%	34.5%
" 10 "	1,264.9	40.9	48.0	46.4	55.6
" 20 "	1,568.5	50.8	59.5	57.5	69.0
" 26 "	1,654.1	53.5	62.7	60.7	72.8
All 43 "	1,654.1	53.5	62.7	60.7	72.8

SOURCES: Text; Iqbal Haidari and Abdul Hafeez Khan, *Stock Exchange Guide of Pakistan*, rev. edn. (Karachi, 1968).

listings by the smaller groups kept the total growth for the 43 groups in line with the growth of all assets on the exchange.

Next, we add the assets of the 36 firms listed exclusively on the Dacca Stock Exchange, of which 6 were controlled by the leading families. Column (2) of Table 4-1 gives these figures for the 43 families and groups. Table 4-5 relates the total assets of the families and groups to the total assets listed on the two exchanges. The concentration rates are lower when assets listed on both exchanges are included. The Karachi Exchange was the major exchange for listing companies from both exchanges. Only the smaller companies from East Pakistan would have listed solely on the Dacca Exchange. Since the companies of the 43 groups had the prestige of the group behind them and most were large enough to warrant listing on the Karachi Exchange, the lower concentration is not surprising.

TABLE 4-5

Percentage Control of All Non-Financial Assets Listed on the Karachi and Dacca Stock Exchanges, 1968 (Rs. million)

	All Assets	All Assets of Privately Controlled Firms	All Assets of Pakistani-Controlled Firms	All Assets of Private Pakistani-Controlled Firms
	Rs.10,963.9	Rs.8,562.9	Rs.10,076.2	Rs.7,675.2
Largest 4 groups Rs.1,957.3	17.8%	22.9%	19.4%	25.5%
" 10 " 3,473.4	31.7	40.6	34.5	45.3
" 20 " 4,495.3	41.0	52.5	44.6	58.6
" 30 " 5,010.7	45.7	58.5	49.7	65.3
All 43 " 5,266.1	48.0	61.5	52.3	68.6

SOURCES: Table 4-1; Appendix to Chapter IV.

We next subtract the assets of listed companies engaged in mining, transportation, gas and electric utilities, construction, storage, and trade. This yields the assets of listed manufacturing firms only. These figures are shown in column (3) of Table 4-1, and the related concentration figures are shown in Table 4-6. These concentration figures are the highest so far. These families and groups have indeed specialized in manufacturing and have left these other activities largely to the government and to other entrepreneurs.

As our final task, we must relate all of the manufacturing assets, including unlisted firms, of the 43 groups to the total of all manufacturing assets in Pakistan in 1968. The results of these calculations are shown in column (4) of Table 4-1 and in Table 4-7. It is important to remember that the base against which these percentages apply is "large-scale" industry (i.e., firms with 20 or more employees or using power); there simply are no good esti-

TABLE 4-6

Percentage Control of All Manufacturing Assets Listed on the Karachi and Dacca Stock Exchanges, 1968 (Rs. million)

	All Assets	All Assets of Privately Controlled Firms	All Assets of Pakistani- Controlled Firms	All Assets of Private Pakistani- Controlled Firms
	Rs.8,531.3	Rs.7,520.5	Rs.7,643.6	Rs.6,632.8
Largest 4 Groups Rs.1,956.4	22.9%	26.0%	25.6%	29.5%
" 10 " 3,333.0	39.1	44.3	43.6	50.3
" 20 " 4,354.0	51.0	57.9	57.0	65.6
" 30 " 4,868.6	57.1	64.7	63.7	73.4
All 43 " 5,124.0	60.1	68.1	67.0	77.3

SOURCES: Table 4-1; Appendix to Chapter IV.

TABLE 4-7

Percentage Control of All Large Scale Manufacturing Assets in Pakistan, 1968. (Rs. million)

	All Assets	All Assets of Privately Controlled Firms	All Assets of Pakistani- Controlled Firms	All Assets of Private Pakistani- Controlled Firms
	Rs.15,059.0	Rs.12,265.0	Rs.13,642.4	Rs.10,848.4
Largest 4 Groups Rs.2,006.3	13.3%	16.4%	14.7%	18.5%
" 10 " 3,547.7	23.6	28.9	26.0	32.7
" 20 " 4,884.4	32.4	39.8	35.8	45.0
" 30 " 5,624.6	37.4	45.9	41.2	51.8
All 43 " 6,314.6	41.9	51.5	46.3	58.2

SOURCES: Table 4-1; Appendix to Chapter IV.

mates available for small-scale and cottage manufacturing. The figures indicate that all 43 families and groups controlled over two-fifths of all large-scale manufacturing and just under three-fifths of all private Pakistani-controlled manufacturing. The 20 largest families and groups controlled almost a third of all manufacturing and 45% of all private Pakistani-controlled manufacturing. These figures are lower than those in the previous tables. Most of the industrial holdings of the leading families were listed on the stock exchanges, whereas there were many moderate-size (but large enough to qualify as "large-scale" for the censuses) unlisted establishments owned and controlled by other entrepreneurs.

The figures in Table 4-7 indicate that the concentration of industrial economic power was high in Pakistan, though not as high as Mahbub ul Haq, cited earlier, claimed to be true. (The figures in Table 4-6, referring just to manufacturing assets listed on the two stock exchanges, would be consistent with Haq's claim, however.) Since these figures involve estimates, especially of the total amount of manfacturing assets in the Pakistani economy, there may well be built-in errors. But even if all of the base estimates for manufacturing assets were actually 25% larger than I estimated, the levels of concentration would still be very high; the 20 largest groups would still control 26% of all manufacturing assets, 36% of all private Pakistani-controlled manufacturing assets; all 43 groups would still control 34% of all manufacturing assets, 47% of private Pakistani-controlled manufacturing assets.

Table 4-8 provides estimates of the geographical control of manufacturing assets. The holdings of the 43 industrial families were not equally split between the two wings of Pakistan. Rather, 72.4% of the families' hold-

TABLE 4-8
Control of Manufacturing Assets, East and West Pakistan, 1968 (Rs. million)

	Assets Controlled by Leading 43 Families (1)	Total Manu- facturing Assets (2)	Total Assets of Privately Controlled Firms (3)	(1) as a % of (2)	(1) as a % of (3)
East Pakistan	Rs.1,740.8	5,581.8	3,859.9	31.2%	45.1%
West Pakistan	4,563.8	9,477.2	8,405.1	48.3	54.4
Total	6,314.6	15,059.0	12,265.0	41.9	51.5
East Pakistan as a % of Total	27.6	37.1	31.5		
West Pakistan as a % of Total	72.4	62.9	68.5		

SOURCES: Appendix to Chapter IV; Table 4A-1; Table 4-7.

ings were in West Pakistan and only 27.6% were in East Pakistan. They also controlled a large percentage of the total manufacturing assets in the west wing, 48.3%, compared to only 31.2% of the total in the east. Further, in Table 4-9, we can see the manufacturing sources of the economic power of the leading 43 groups. Over 40% of the assets of these groups came from cotton textiles and jute, over 65% from those two industries plus chemicals and sugar.

The primary focus of this study is on the leading Pakistani industrial families. There were, however, 7 large foreign-controlled firms that would have qualified, on the basis of their assets sizes, to be included in the list in Table 4-1. The 2 largest foreign firms were the Pakistan Tobacco Co., accounting for Rs.252.9 million in assets and controlled by the British-American Tobacco Company of Great Britain, and the Esso Pakistan Fertilizer Company, accounting for Rs.224.1 million in assets and

TABLE 4-9

Control of Manufacturing Assets, by Industry, 1968 (Rs. million)

	Assets Controlled	% of Total Holdings by 43 Families
Cotton textiles	Rs.1,707.8	27.0%
Jute textiles	1,004.1	15.9
Chemicals	763.2	12.1
Sugar	696.6	11.0
Petroleum	464.9	7.4
Cement	360.5	5.7
Steel and metal manufacturing	271.6	4.3
Paper	263.8	4.2
Wool and artificial silk-textiles	169.8	2.7
Vehicle assembly	133.1	2.1
Vegetable ghee	119.2	1.9
Miscellaneous food	53.8	0.9
Miscellaneous	306.2	4.8
Total	6,314.6	100.0

SOURCE: See text.

controlled by the Standard Oil Company of New Jersey. In an expanded list of 50 domestic and foreign families and organizations, these 7 foreign-controlled companies would have ranked seventh, tenth, twentieth, thirty-third, forty-first, forty-sixth, and forty-eighth by size of assets.

Table 4-10 presents the concentration figures for this expanded domestic-foreign list, compared to all manufacturing assets and all privately controlled manufacturing assets. The inclusion of the foreign-controlled firms raises the control of the 10 leading organizations to 24.2% of all manufacturing assets and to 29.7% of all privately controlled manufacturing assets. The figures for the 20 leading organizations are raised to 34.3% and

TABLE 4-10

Percentage Control, Including Leading Foreign Firms, of All Large-Scale Manufacturing Assets in Pakistan, 1968 (Rs. million)

	All Assets Rs.15,059.0	All Assets of Privately Controlled Firms Rs.12,265.0
Largest 4 families and organizations Rs.2,006.3	13.3%	16.4%
" 10 " " " 3,646.7	24.2	29.7
" 20 " " " 5,164.2	34.3	42.1
" 30 " " " 5,978.5	39.7	48.7
All 50 " " " 7,123.1	47.3	58.1

SOURCES: Table 4-1; State Bank of Pakistan, *Balance Sheet Analysis of Joint Stock Companies Listed on the Karachi Stock Exchange, 1964-69* (Karachi, 1971).

42.1%, respectively. The figures for all 50 organizations are 47.3% and 58.1% respectively.

Overall Concentration—Some Comparisons

Economics has no model for concentration in the large that is analogous to the model of competition relevant for concentration in a single industry. One can only say that less concentration is surely better than more, but we have no way of telling whether 50 organizations controlling 50% of manufacturing assets, or 500 organizations, or 50,000 is a reasonably satisfactory situation. I will argue in Chapter 7, however, that the actual level of overall concentration had serious economic and political-social consequences for Pakistan, and in that sense it was too high.

We can get some idea of relative magnitudes by making comparisons over time and across countries. If the figures in Table 4-10 are compared to Papanek's estimates for 1959 (which also included foreign firms), they indicate that there was virtually no decline in overall concentration during the 1960's. The Pakistani manufacturing sector grew rapidly, but so did the large families and foreign firms.

When we turn to international comparisons, we confront a number of measurement hazards. If manufacturing is the sector in which concentration is to be compared, is manufacturing consistently defined among the countries to be compared? Are government-controlled and foreign-controlled firms consistently included or excluded? Are the base figures consistently all manufacturing firms listed on a stock exchange, all manufacturing corporations, or all manufacturing firms? Further, are the comparisons consistently based on assets controlled? The largest firms in an economy will probably be the same, whether measured by assets or by labor force, but large firms tend to be more capital-intensive than small firms. Hence, their concentration will be greater if measured by assets than if measured by labor force, and comparisons using one measure in one country and the other in another may introduce severe bias. These consistency requirements serve to restrict the field of available comparisons but do not eliminate them entirely.

Hazari has made estimates similar to those of this study for industrial control in India for 1958.[20] His concept of the "inner circle" of holdings of industrial groups is comparable to my concept of control. His figures for the percentages of the assets of non-government industrial companies controlled by the largest 4, 13, and 20 groups are presented in Table 4-11, along with the comparable Pakistani figures for 1968. The shares controlled by the

[20] E. K. Hazari, *The Corporate Private Sector* (Bombay, 1966).

TABLE 4-11

A Comparison of Percentage Control of the Assets of Privately
Controlled Industrial Firms, India and Pakistan

	Publicly Listed Companies Only[a]		Public & Private Companies[b]	
	India (1958)	Pakistan (1968)	India (1958)	Pakistan (1968)
Largest 4 groups	22.1%	22.9%	17.2%	16.4%
" 13 "	30.5	47.7	26.2	34.1
" 20 "	32.2	56.6	28.0	42.1

[a] Both the India and Pakistan figures refer to the assets of industrial firms.

[b] The figures for India refer to the assets of industrial firms, whereas the figures for Pakistan refer to the assets of manufacturing firms only.

SOURCES: Tables 4-5 and 4-10; E. K. Hazari, *The Corporate Private Sector* (Bombay, 1966), ch. 2.

leading 4 groups are about the same in Pakistan and India, but Pakistan's concentration is considerably greater when the largest 13 and 20 groups are considered.

For Chile, Petras has estimated that 9 firms control 25% of total industrial capital.[21] He is not explicit, however, as to the base for his estimate, but one can conclude that the figures for the 10 leading families and organizations in Table 4-10 are definitely in the same range as this estimate for Chile.

In the United States, there has been concern over recent Federal Trade Commission figures indicating that the share of the 100 largest corporations in the country had grown to just under 50% of all manufacturing assets. For the 53 leading corporations in the U.S., the figure

[21] James Petras, *Politics and Social Forces in Chilean Development* (Berkeley, 1969), p. 52.

was 38%.[22] In Pakistan, the 50 leading families and organizations controlled 47%. For the United Kingdom, Florence reports that the 100 largest industrial and commercial companies in the early 1950's accounted for 29% of all company (corporate) business activity and 20% of all business activity (including partnerships and sole proprietorships).[23] In Germany, the 50 leading industrial companies in 1966 accounted for 38.9% of the sales of all industry.[24] In Japan, the 3 leading Zaibatsu groups controlled between 7% and 17% of the paid-in capital of all Japanese corporations in 1960.[25] In Sweden, one family is reported to control 8 of the 10 largest industrial firms.[26]

It is difficult to know what to conclude from these few international comparisons.[27] At first thought, one might

[22] U.S. Federal Trade Commission, *Economic Report on Corporate Mergers* (Washington, 1970), pp. 168, 173.

[23] P. Sargant Florence, *Ownership, Control, and Success of Large Companies* (London, 1961), pp. 9-12.

[24] Helmut Arndt, Testimony in *Economic Concentration*, Part 7, hearings before the Subcommittee on Antitrust and Monopoly, Committee on the Judiciary, U.S. Senate (Washington, D.C., 1968), p. 3,490.

[25] Eugene Rotwein, "Economic Concentration and Monopoly in Japan," *Journal of Political Economy* (June 1964).

[26] "The Wallenberg Boys—And How They Grew," *Business Week* (February 25, 1967).

[27] The comparisons, based on the *numbers* of leading groups, overstate the concentration in a small country like Pakistan, in the following sense. There were slightly over 5,000 large-scale manufacturing organizations in Pakistan in 1967-1968, so 50 groups represented 0.1%. There were over 300,000 manufacturing firms in the U.S. in 1967, so the 50 largest firms represented 0.0016%. In terms of the *percentage* of firms that control a given percentage of industrial assets, the U.S. is far more concentrated. But the economic and political-social consequences are likely

argue that overall economic concentration would be inversely related to the absolute size of a country's industrial sector. Hence, it would be "natural" that Pakistan would have a higher rate of overall concentration than, say, the United States or India. But this would be true only if all three of the following propositions were true for all countries: (1) the technological dictates of size of firm (by industry) are the same; (2) the percentage distribution of industries is the same; and (3) the rules and laws on mergers and multi-company control are the same. Since none of these three is generally true, the hypothesized relationship need not hold. If Pakistan had encouraged more labor-intensive technologies and had operated its foreign exchange system in a less restrictive manner (see Chapter 6), its level of overall concentration might have been considerably less.

Further, it is important to note that any given corporate concentration level in the United States has a less severe effect on the distribution of income and wealth than is true for Pakistan. The shares of most U.S. corporations are widely held, whereas even the shares of Pakistani companies listed on the Karachi Stock Exchange tended to be owned mostly by a small group of insiders. The power consequences of economic concentration, though, remain as valid for the non-owner managers in the U.S. as for the family-owner manager in Pakistan.

Finally, the levels of overall manufacturing concentration in the U.S., Germany, Great Britain, and other Western European countries appear to have increased in recent years and are certainly higher than they were 80 to 100 years ago. There seems to be no guarantee that the

---

to flow from the economic power residing in individual firms and groups, not from percentages, so the concentration by *numbers* of firms are the relevant figures here.

increase in the size of an industrial sector over time will automatically mean a decrease in overall concentration.

What, then, does one conclude from these few international comparisons? Overall concentration in manufacturing seems to be greater in Pakistan than in India, the United States, and Germany, about the same as in Chile and Japan, and may be somewhat less than in Sweden. Concentration of economic power in Pakistan is certainly not a unique phenomenon—but that does not make it any less worthy of concern.

Banking

The positions of some of these families were further buttressed by their control of banks and insurance companies. It is to these figures that we now turn.

At the end of 1968 there were 23 domestically controlled banks and 20 foreign-controlled banks operating in Pakistan. These banks had total assets or liabilities of Rs.24,178 million. Total earning assets were Rs.14,259.5 million, and total deposits were Rs.12,558.1 million. Since banks are the markets for both receiving money (deposits) and lending money (earning assets), concentration in both markets will be discussed.

As shown in Table 4-12, the first, third, and fourth largest banks were controlled by industrial families: Habib, Saigol, and Adamjee. (The number after the family name in the table is the family's industrial ranking.) The second largest bank was controlled by the Central Government.[28] Together, the 4 largest banks had over three-fourths of total deposits and just under two-thirds of earning assets. The 3 largest private banks by

[28] A smaller bank, the Bank of Bahawalpur, is a subsidiary of the National Bank of Pakistan, but it is operated separately.

TABLE 4-12

Control in Banking, December 1968

	Deposits		Earning Assets	
	Amount (Rs. million)	% of total	Amount (Rs. million)	% of total
Total banking system	Rs.12,558.1	100.0%	Rs.14,259.5	100.0%
Total private domestic banks	8,270.6	65.9	8,335.0	58.4
Total government banks	3,039.5	24.2	4,501.2	31.6
Total foreign banks	1,248.0	9.9	1,423.3	10.0
Largest four banks:				
Habib Bank (Habib, 13)	3,443.0	27.4	3,123.0	21.9
National Bank of Pakistan				
(Government)	2,678.7	21.3	2,970.4	20.8
United Bank (Saigol, 2)	2,384.6	19.0	2,140.1	15.0
Muslim Commercial Bank				
(Adamjee, 3)	1,116.4	8.9	1,093.6	7.7
Total	9,622.0	76.6	9,327.1	65.4
Largest 3 private banks	6,944.0	55.3	6,356.7	44.6
Other banks owned by				
industrial families:	295.2			
Commerce Bank (Fancy, 6)	295.2	2.4	392.7	2.8
Australasia Bank (Shaikh, 5)	285.7	2.3	285.1	2.0
Memon Cooperative Bank				
(Dawood, 1) (est.)	40.0	0.3	n.a.	–
Premier Bank (Arag, 18)	7.4	–	2.0	–
Total, 7 family banks	7,572.3	60.3	7,036.5	49.3
7 family banks as % of				
total less government	79.6%		72.1%	
7 family banks as % of				
total less foreign	67.0%		54.8%	
7 family banks as % of				
private Pakistani-				
controlled total	91.6%		84.4%	

SOURCE: State Bank of Pakistan, *Banking Statistics of Pakistan, 1968-69* (Karachi, 1971).

themselves had over half of total deposits and a little under half of total earning assets.

Four other industrial family groups controlled banks: Fancy, Shaikh, Dawood, and Haji Habib (Arag). The 7 banks controlled by these 7 industrial families accounted for 60.3% of all bank deposits in Pakistan. If the deposits of government-controlled banks and foreign banks are excluded, these 7 banks accounted for 91.6% of all deposits. On the other side of the ledger, these banks accounted for 84.4% of all earning assets of private Pakistani-controlled banks.

These are high rates of concentration, particularly considering the fact that these are nationwide figures. Not all banks have branches in all localities, and thus the local rates of concentration must be higher. When this banking concentration is combined with the overall concentration estimated above, the scope for generating large amounts of economic and political power becomes wide indeed.

There are two possible mitigating circumstances. First, the government-controlled National Bank of Pakistan might have pursued an aggressive expansionary policy and by its actions limited the power of the private banks. Second, the banking system was regulated by the central government, and an ideal regulatory regime might have kept the power of the banks in check. In practice, however, the National Bank of Pakistan has not been particularly outstanding in its behavior. Rather, the opinion of many Pakistani businessmen is that the National Bank has behaved more or less in a pattern similar to that of the other commercial banks. Also, the regulatory regime was far from ideal. The general policy of the banking authorities was to set low interest rates on loans and yet lower rates on deposits. The profit-and-loss statements and balance sheets of the banks indicate that they were able to make quite healthy profits under this arrangement. The low interest rates on loans meant that demand for these loans exceeded the available supply, and the banks had to ration loans among their customers. Those individuals who were fortunate enough to get these loans benefitted greatly, and these loans were going primarily to the large industrial families and groups.

Further, there is some evidence that the family banks tended to give some favor to the industrial companies owned by the same families. The State Bank compilation of balance sheets of listed companies indicates which banks these companies primarily dealt with. In virtually all cases, banks controlled by industrial families were one of the 2 to 4 banks listed by the industrial companies controlled by those same families. It is most unlikely that this was coincidence.

Insurance

The insurance industry is less concentrated and considerably smaller in overall size than banking. At the end of 1968 there were 46 Pakistani-owned insurance companies with total assets of Rs.850.6 million in life and general insurance; there were also 32 foreign-owned companies with Rs.472.9 million in assets. Of the total assets of Rs.1,323.5 million, about 79% represented earning assets. The financial size of the industry, then, if measured by earning assets, was less than a tenth of that of the banking industry. Nevertheless, public concern about the insurance industry, not only on questions concerning the costs and terms of insurance policies but also on questions of the financial power of the insurance companies, has been equal to or greater than the concern about the banking industry. Nationalization of the insurance industry has been a frequently discussed issue. I believe that this is an example of the importance of the urban population in shaping political issues. Virtually all insurance is sold in the urban areas, and its impact on the urban middle class is probably stronger than that of the banking sector, which has most of its dealings with business. Thus the relative importance of the insurance industry in the eyes of the urban middle class far exceeds its relative asset size.

The first and third largest insurance companies were controlled by industrial families: Haji Habib (Arag) and Habib. The second and fourth were foreign-owned. Together, these 4 controlled 53% of all the assets in the insurance industry.

In addition to the 2 family firms in the top 4, another 12 insurance companies were controlled by industrial families or groups. These figures are shown in Table 4-13, along with the controlling family and its industrial ranking. These companies controlled Rs.642.7 million or 48.6% of all assets; this figure also represented 75.6% of all assets controlled by Pakistani-controlled firms.

Aside from the Eastern Federal and Habib Insurance Companies, the sizes of the insurance companies controlled by industrial families and groups were small compared to the industrial assets controlled by these same groups. Only for the Haji Habib (Arag) and Habib families were the insurance assets larger than the industrial assets.

The portfolios of these industrial family-controlled insurance companies tended to favor companies controlled by the same groups. Most insurance companies invested in a wide variety of industrial companies. But the percentages of the stock portfolios of industrial family insurance companies devoted to the shares of the companies of those families generally exceeded the percentages of these companies' total assets compared to the total assets of all industrial companies traded on the stock exchanges. This is seen in Table 4-14. In only a few

TABLE 4-13

Control of Insurance Assets, 1968 (Rs. million)

	Assets	Percent
46 Pakistani insurers	Rs. 850.6	64.3%
32 Foreign insurers	472.9	35.7
Total	1,323.5	100.0
Eastern Federal (Arag, 18)	Rs. 271.6	20.5
American Life (foreign)	187.4	14.2
Habib (Habib, 13)	136.6	10.3
Norwich Union (foreign)	105.5	8.0
Total	701.1	53.0
New Jubilee (Fancy, 6)	Rs. 57.3	4.3
Adamjee (Adamjee, 3)	49.6	3.7
Premier (Bashir, 9)	35.5	2.7
Central (Dawood, 1)	21.4	1.6
United (Valika, 7)	14.7	1.1
Eastern (A. K. Khan, 29)	12.6	1.0
International General (Wazir Ali, 10)	10.5	0.8
Khyber (Khyber, 14)	8.6	0.7
Crescent Star (Millwala, 21)	8.3	0.6
National Security (Shaikh, 5)	7.3	0.6
Union (Nishat, 15)	5.7	0.4
Universal (Ghandara, 11)	3.0	0.2
Total, all industrial family insurance companies	642.7	48.6
Total as % of Pakistani insurance companies		75.6

SOURCE: Controller of Insurance, *Pakistan Insurance Yearbook, 1969* (Karachi, 1970), pp. 31-32, 297-307, 479-495.

instances, though, did the share ownership of an industrial company by an insurance company exceed 10% of the industrial company's shares. Thus, the insurance company investments seem to have been less oriented toward gaining control of industrial companies and more toward providing a ready market for some of the family's

TABLE 4-14

Family-Controlled Insurance Companies' Holdings of Own Family-Controlled Industrial Companies, 1968

	% of Portfolios Invested in Family Industrial Companies	Family Industrial Assets as a % of All Assets Listed on Karachi and Dacca Exchanges
Eastern Federal (Arag)	3.9%	0.3%
Habib (Habib)	20.1	1.2
New Jubilee (Fancy)	21.6	2.6
Adamjee (Adamjee)	19.9	4.1
Premier (Bashir)	14.4	1.8
Central (Dawood)	19.2	5.1
United (Valika)	31.6	2.9
Eastern (A. K. Khan)	25.9	0.2
International General (Wazir Ali)	0	1.2
Khyber (Khyber)	0	1.2
Crescent Star (Millwala)	0	0
National Security (Shaikh)	92.4	3.0
Union (Nishat)	62.3	0.6
Universal (Ghandara)	0	1.4

SOURCES: Table 4-1; Controller of Insurance, *Pakistan Insurance Yearbook, 1969* (Karachi, 1970), pp. 231-295, 497-561.

shares when the family wished to sell some of its shares without depressing the prices of the shares of its companies. Only at the end of 1970 did the central government finally promulgate an ordinance forbidding insurance companies from making investments in companies in which the directors of the insurance company had an interest, except with the prior approval of the central government. The insurance companies also appear to have favored banks owned by the same families by keeping their time deposits in those banks.

Interlocking Directorates

The major industrial families and entrepreneurs were no strangers to each other. Some were members of the same religious sects or communities.[29] Some had marriage ties through children or cousins of the original "founding father" industrialists. Members of the families tended to sit on each other's boards of directors. They also sat on the boards of companies outside of the group of 43 that have been analyzed. The influence of the industrial families and groups clearly extended beyond their own companies.

Table 4-15 shows the results of the pattern of interlocking directorates.[30] There were 103 cases in which one family had at least one member on the board of directors of at least one company of another family. Some families were represented on more than one company of another family, so a total of 146 company interlocks were found.[31] In addition, there were 103 instances of family members sitting on the boards of listed companies not controlled by the 43 groups under discussion.

It is difficult to determine a base to which the 146 family interlocks should be compared. There are 1,806 possible interlocks among the 43 families. But 4 of the

[29] See Papanek, *Pakistan's Development*, Ch. 2; and Hannah Papanek, "Pakistan's Big Businessmen: Muslim Separation, Entrepreneurship and Partial Modernization," *Economic Development and Cultural Change* (October 1972).

[30] For recent work on interlocking directorates in the U.S., see Peter C. Dooley, "The Interlocking Directorate," *American Economic Review* (June 1969); and W. Lloyd Warner, Darab B. Unwalla, and John H. Trimm, *The Emergent American Society*, Vol. I (New Haven, 1967), Ch. 5.

[31] In cases in which two members of the same family sit on the board of a single company of another family, only one interlock is recorded.

TABLE 4-15

Corporate Interlocks Among the Leading Industrial Families, 1968

(1)	Number of Families on Boards of Directors of Family in Column (1) (2)	Representation of Family in Column (1) on other Families' Boards of Directors (3)	Representation of Family in Column (1) on Boards of Directors of Non-Family Firms (4)
1. Dawood	8	8	8
2. Saigol	3	6	3
3. Adamjee	11	8	9
4. Jalil	8	6	–
5. Shaikh	8	3	–
6. Fancy	4	1	9
7. Valika	7	2	4
8. Bawany	3	6	5
9. Bashir	4	9	7
10. Wazir Ali	1	1	5
11. Ghandara	1	5	6
12. Ispahani	–	4	1
13. Habib	6	6	3
14. Khyber Textile Group	–	4	2
15. Nishat Group	2	2	3
16. BECO	1	–	–
17. Gul Ahmed	–	1	1
18. Arag	4	8	4
19. Hafiz	–	1	2
20. H. A. Karim	–	–	–
21. Millwala	–	3	1
22. Hyesons	2	8	4
23. Dada	–	20	9
24. Premier Group	–	–	–
25. Hussein Ebrahim	3	5	1
26. Monnoo	1	1	–
27. Maulabaksh	–	1	1
28. Adam	2	–	–
29. A. K. Khan	1	2	2
30. A. A. Ghani	–	7	2

TABLE 4-15 (Continued)

(1)	Number of Families on Boards of Directors of Family in Column (1) (2)	Representation of Family in Column (1) on other Families' Boards of Directors (3)	Representation of Family in Column (1) on Boards of Directors of Non-Family Firms (4)
31. Rangoonwala	7	5	4
32. Haroon	1	–	3
33. Hirgina	–	–	–
34. Shaffi	3	2	1
35. Fakir Chand	–	–	–
36. Haji Hashan	1	–	–
37. Dadabhoy	–	6	1
38. Shahnawaz	2	1	–
39. Fateh Textile Group	–	–	–
40. Noon	–	–	–
41. Hoti	–	4	2
42. Ghulam Faruque	5	1	–
43. Haji Dost Mohd.	1	–	–
Total[a]	103	146	103

[a] The total in column (3) is larger than that of column (2) because the former counts the memberships of a given family on the boards of directors of more than one company of another family.

SOURCES: State Bank of Pakistan, *Balance Sheet Analysis of Joint Stock Companies Listed on the Karachi Stock Exchange, 1964-69* (Karachi, 1971); Iqbal Haidari and Abdul Hafeez Khan, *Stock Exchange Guide of Pakistan*, rev. edn. (Karachi, 1968).

families did not have any publicly listed companies, so that reduces the number of possible interlocks to 1,466. Further, many families had only 2 or 3 listed companies. There were an average of 6 or 7 directors on each board, and 2 or 3 of these usually came from the controlling families. Hence, it was physically impossible for all families to be represented on the boards of all other families.

There were 115 companies controlled by the 43 groups listed on the Karachi Stock Exchange.[32] The 146 company interlocks represents an average of 1.3 interlocks per company. This means that about one-third of the seats on boards of directors of companies controlled by the 43 groups that were not occupied by the controlling family were occupied by members of other families within the 43.

Table 4-15 indicates that there was a tendency for the more important families to have more representation on their own companies' boards by other families and also a tendency, though weaker, for the more important families to place more of their members on the boards of other families.[33] In addition, the more important fam-

---

[32] There were 98 industrial companies, 5 banks, and 12 insurance companies.

[33] This is shown by the following statistics: Let us multiply the number of families that are represented on a particular family's boards (column 2) by the industrial ranking of the family (column 1); i.e., multiply 8 (the number of families represented on Dawood company boards) by 1 (the Dawood industrial ranking), 3 (families on Saigol companies) by 2 (the Saigol ranking), and so on. The sum of these products is 1,481. If the 103 interlocks had been distributed evenly around the mid-point of the family distribution (i.e., around the twenty-Saigol ranking), and so on. The sum of these products is 1,481. 2,266. The lower summed products indicate that the more important families tended to have more families on their boards. The 1,481 summed products are equivalent to the 103 interlocks distributing themselves equally around the fourteenth-ranking family. Similarly, the summed products for the representation of a given family on other family boards are 2,523. This is equivalent to the 146 interlocks distributing themselves equally around the seventeenth-ranking family.

ilies tended to be more represented on the boards of non-family companies.[34]

The inclusion of a member of an important family on the board of another company was frequently just for show, a token to give the company prestige. The family member may not have taken an active role in that company's affairs. Yet even this desire to have family members on boards is an indication of the potential power of the important industrial families.

The influence of the important families did not stop here. They were frequently on the boards of government corporations and agencies, which in turn had the power to influence government decisions with respect to licenses and quotas for the companies controlled by the families. A more thorough discussion of this point is given in Chapter 7 on the effect of this concentration of economic power.

[34] A summed product calculation gives a figure that is equivalent to all 103 outside directorships distributing themselves equally around the fourteenth-ranking family.

Chapter 5

Concentration by Industry

IF one wishes to explore the causes and effects of monopoly and market power, one needs to know where it exists. This requires information on market structure and concentration in individual industries. This kind of information has become a regular part of the statistics yielded by the periodic industrial censuses in many developed countries, but it is not available for most LDC's. This chapter attempts to develop a picture of the market structure of a large number of industries in Pakistan.

This chapter first presents a brief discussion of the problems and pitfalls of trying to measure concentration in individual industries and will explain the sources and methods used in this study. Then, the Pakistani concentration figures are presented and evaluated, and some comparisons to United States figures are provided. The position of the 43 leading families and groups within the major concentrated industries is noted. A discussion of monopoly in retailing concludes the chapter.

Defining Markets and Concentration

Economists feel much more confident in discussing concentration by industry than concentration across the entire manufacturing sector. Here, their models are reasonably well worked out, at least for static analysis, with the welfare implications of different market structures fairly well agreed upon.

Despite the economist's comfort with the concept of concentration by industry, actual measurement of concentration can create severe discomfort. First, one has to define the relevant market in which one tries to measure concentration. The textbook model of a market applies strictly to a uniform product. But is it meaningful to study only the market for single-edged razor blades if moderate price changes will shift demand significantly to or from double-edged blades and also cause producers to shift their production significantly between the two products? Clearly not.[1] Therefore, one has to include close substitutes (in both consumption and production) in one's study of a market. But how close is close and where does one draw the line? In the end, one can only be pragmatic and draw the line where it seems appropriate and hope that most observers will agree.[2]

Second, to what geographical area are we referring? For easily transported items, national concentration figures are meaningful. But if products have high domestic transport costs, local producers may be effectively buffered from competitors elsewhere in the country, and national concentration figures may understate the true concentration picture at the local level.

Third, on what basis should we measure concentration? Value added, sales (or production), employment,

[1] Substitution can also occur on just one side of the market or the other. For example, cane sugar and beet sugar are virtually perfect substitutes for consumers, though there is little substitutability in production. And it is easy for producers to substitute the production of wood screws for stove bolts, but there is little substitution by consumers.

[2] For a further discussion of this and related points, see F. M. Scherer, *Industrial Market Structure and Economic Performance*, pp. 53-57; and Leonard Weiss, "Average Concentration Ratios and Industrial Performance," *Journal of Industrial Economics* (July 1963).

or physical capacity are all possible bases. Sales, for example, would provide a measure of actual market power; capacity would provide a measure of potential market power.

Fourth, what measure of concentration should we use? The percentage of the market controlled by the 4 largest firms is a convenient and frequently used measure, but it ignores distributional differences among the first 4 and it ignores any information on the other firms in the market. Besides, 4 is a wholly arbitrary number; why not 5 or 8 or 17? A measure based on a Lorenz curve frequency distribution (the Gini coefficient) makes fuller use of market information, but that is also its weakness: it requires complete information about market shares. Also, it fails to distinguish between a market structure in which 2 firms equally share a market and one in which 100 firms equally share the market. The Herfindahl index (the sum of the squares of the market shares) appears to be the best compromise, but, like the Gini coefficient, it requires complete market shares information.[3]

The Measures Used

In trying to measure industrial concentration in Pakistan, I have had to confront all four points. I have tried wherever possible to define product markets narrowly, primarily because of the lack of ease of substitution on

---

[3] For a more extended discussion of concentration measures, see Scherer, *op.cit.*, pp. 50-52; John Perry Miller, "Measures of Monopoly Power and Concentration: Their Economic Significance," in *Business Concentration and Price Policy*, National Bureau of Economic Research (Princeton, 1955); and Morris A. Adelman, "Comment on the 'H' Concentration Measure as a Numbers-Equivalent," *Review of Economics and Statistics* (February 1969).

the production side. Most of the capital equipment and raw materials for industrial production are imported. Pakistan's import licensing system restricted access to these imports and thus made it difficult for entrepreneurs to shift their production from one output to another. Accordingly, rather than define a "chemicals" industry, I have given separate figures for caustic soda, soda ash, etc. Not only is it difficult for consumers to substitute among these products but producers of these chemicals simply cannot switch easily from one to the other.

Wherever possible, I have defined the industrial concentration information on an all-Pakistan basis. For many industries, though, the only information available on concentration was for West Pakistan alone, and in those cases I have reported only these ratios. Since the bulk of the manufacturing in these industries did in fact take place in West Pakistan, not too much information is lost by this procedure. Over 80% of production in East Pakistan in 1968 was accounted for by food, tobacco, textiles, paper, and leather. Around 70% of the inter-wing trade from East to West in 1967-1968 consisted of tea, jute textiles, other textiles, and paper—industries for which good figures on an all-Pakistan basis are available —and much of the remainder was in raw materials. Manufacturing in West Pakistan was not threatened by much competition from East Pakistan.

Sales data were used as the basis for measurement in the few cases where it was possible. In the remaining cases, capacity data was used. Unfortunately, capacity data in Pakistan has a rubbery aspect to it. Capacity can be variously defined as "operating" capacity (assuming the same number of shifts per factory), "installed" capacity (including that which has yet to be put into operation or is idle for want of spare parts), or "installed and sanctioned" capacity (which includes the capacity that may have been approved by the national investment sanctioning agencies but that has yet to be installed or sometimes is not yet even ordered). Sometimes writers neglect to mention which concept they are referring to, and comparisons become problematical. Also, there may be a tendency for firms to overstate their capacity to any statistical collection agency, since imported raw materials allocations are frequently based on capacity. Nevertheless, capacity was the only measure available by firm in most industries, and, despite its limitations, it provided the basis for most of the industry concentration ratios. The source for most of these capacity figures was the *Directory of Industrial Establishments in West Pakistan*.[4] The compilers of this directory made an effort to assess the installed capacity of all firms, so comparisons of firms within an industry are possible. They also tried to include unregistered firms in their survey. Other sources included textile yearbooks, the Central Statistical Office's *Monthly Statistical Bulletin*, and special studies of vegetable ghee (shortening) and cigarettes in West Pakistan.[5]

Finally, four-firm concentration ratios were chosen, mainly because of their convenience and minimum information requirements.[6] In cases in which a family or

[4] Government of West Pakistan, *Directory of Industrial Establishments* (Lahore, 1969).

[5] Saeed Hafeez, *Textile Yearbook* (Karachi, 1970); Ameen K. Tareen, ed., *Directory of Pakistan Cotton Textile Industry* (Karachi, 1970); Mansur Ahmad, "Vegetable Ghee Industry in West Pakistan," Directorate of Industries and Commerce, Government of West Pakistan (Lahore, 1969); and K. S. Hassan, "Cigarette Manufacturing Industry in West Pakistan," Directorate of Industries and Commerce, Government of West Pakistan (Lahore, 1969).

[6] American data indicate that all the alternative measures of

group controlled more than one firm in an industry, the sales or capacity of the summed holdings were treated as one firm.

The Extent of Industrial Concentration

The results of my efforts to measure industrial concentration in Pakistan are provided in Tables 5-1 and 5-2. Unfortunately, information was not available to make concentration estimates for all industries. Table 5-1 covers the 23 industries for which all-Pakistan estimates could be made. These 23 industries accounted for at least 58.3% of manufacturing value added on an all-Pakistan basis. More information was available for West Pakistan alone, and concentration estimates were made for an additional 59 industries accounting for 16.0% of manufacturing value added in West Pakistan. These are shown in Table 5-2. If we can assume that the figures in Table 5-2 are roughly equivalent to what we would find with more complete data for all Pakistan,[7] the two tables together cover 74.3% of manufacturing value added in Pakistan. Another 5%-10% could probably be attributed to the additional industries for which concentration estimates were possible but for which value added figures were unavailable. Accordingly, even though we could not obtain concentration ratios for every industry in Pakistan, the figures in Table 5-1 and 5-2 are fairly comprehensive, covering over four-fifths of value added in manufacturing.

---

concentration tend to be very highly correlated. See Scherer, *op.cit.*, p. 52.

[7] In terms of value added, at least, this does not appear to be a bad assumption. In Table 5-1, the industries covered accounted for 58.3% of value added in all Pakistan manufacturing. These same industries accounted for 58.0% of value added of West Pakistan manufacturing.

TABLE 5-1

Concentration by Industry, All Pakistan, 1968

Industry	No. of Factories[a]	Shipments	Capacity	% by Largest 4 Firms or Groups	% of Manufacturing Value Added (1967-68) All Pakistan
Cotton spinning	139 (114)		2,812,000 spindles	20%	17.6%
Cotton weaving	90 (79)		35,000 looms	32	3.3
Cotton ginning	401		n.a.	10[b]	0.5
Knitting	260		n.a.	10[b]	
Dying, bleaching, and finishing	270		n.a.	10[b]	0.6
Jute textiles	44 (39)		20,000 looms	37	7.2
Wool textiles	32		60,000	48	1.3
Artificial silk textiles	385		13,000 power looms	10	2.3
Rayon yarn	2	9,000,000 lbs.		100	1.4
Nylon yarn	4		1,000 tons	100	
Cigarettes	20 (14)	35 billion cigarettes		92	4.5
Sugar	27 (18)	378,000 tons		48	4.6
Vegetable ghee	21 (19)	96,000 tons		45	2.3
Tea blending	9 (7)		n.a.	99	2.1

TABLE 5-1 (*Continued*)
Concentration by Industry, All Pakistan, 1968

Industry	No. of Factories[a]	Shipments	Capacity	% by Largest 4 Firms or Groups	% of Manufacturing Value Added (1967-68) All Pakistan
Paper and paperboard	4	78,000 tons	55,250 tons	100	1.9
Caustic soda	4	23,000 tons		100	
Soda ash	2	57,000 tons		100	1.2
Sulfuric acid	4	30,000 tons		100	
Cycle tires	7		2.6 million		
Cycle tubes			9.8 million	95	0.7
Motor vehicle tires	4		105,000 tires	100	
Motor vehicle tubes			210,000 tubes		
Cement	10 (6)		2.8 million tons	86	2.7
Fertilizer	5 (3)	293,000 tons		100	1.8
Petroleum refining	4		5 million tons	100	2.3
			Total		58.3

[a] The number in parentheses excludes multiple factories owned by a company and multiple companies controlled by a family or group.

[b] Exact figures are not available, but these are good estimates.

Source: See text.

TABLE 5-2

Concentration by Industry, West Pakistan, 1968

Industry	No. of Factories	Capacity	% by Largest 4 Firms or Groups	% of Manu- facturing, Value Added, West Pakistan
Rice milling	130	1,000 tons/day	12%	0.1%
Wheat and grain milling	86	7,130 tons/day	14	0.6
Edible oil	183	1,110 expellers	9	ᵃ
Solvent oil extraction	8	145,000 tons	72	ᵃ
Shoes	120	50.2 million pair	41	1.1
Tanning	76	60 million lbs.	30	1.5
Artificial leather cloth	11	6.8 million yards	63	n.a.
Carpets	76	3,730 looms	33	0.4
Canvas	10	276 looms	56	n.a.
Paint	31	45,000 tons	30	0.6
Ink	22	4.8 million lbs.	56	n.a.
Soap and detergents	141	118,800 tons	36	0.7
Cosmetics	68	Rs.37 million	46 ⎱	0.3
Toothpaste	7	52 million tubes	74 ⎰	
Lubricating oils and greases	4	31,000 tons	100	n.a.
Starch	4	29,000 tons	100	n.a.
Glucose	4	10,100 tons	100	n.a.
Ammonium chloride	2	660 tons	100	n.a.
Bleaching powder	2	4,320 tons	100	n.a.
Distillery	8	4.4 million gals.	82	n.a.
Glycerine	5	2,700 tons	91	n.a.
Sulfur refining	4	6,500 tons	100	n.a.
Hydrochloric acid	3	15,700 tons	100	n.a.
Formaldehyde	1	5,000 tons	100	n.a.
Carbon dioxide	6	2.3 million lbs.	91	n.a.
Oxygen	4	130 million cu. ft.	100	n.a.
Acetylene	4	36 million cu. ft.	100	n.a.
Steel foundries	10	84,000 tons	65 ⎱	3.3
Steel rerolling	112	550,000 tons	34 ⎰	

TABLE 5-2 (*Continued*)
Concentration by Industry, West Pakistan, 1968

Industry	No. of Factories	Capacity	% by Largest 4 Firms or Groups	% of Manufacturing, Value Added, West Pakistan
Conduit pipe	11	20 million feet	86 ⎫	
G.I. pipe	12	50,000 tons	82 ⎬	0.2
M.S. pipe	10	15,600 tons	82 ⎭	
Ferrous wire	7	56,000 tons	87 ⎫	
Non-ferrous wire	7	15,500 tons	87 ⎬	0.2
Barbed wire	5	4,000 tons	82 ⎭	
Nails	36	24,000 tons	43 ⎫	0.2
Wood screws	11	3.8 million gross	80 ⎭	
Steel furniture	16	Rs.5.5 million	51	n.a.
Metal cans	54	92,000 tons	35	0.5
Razor blades	4	400 million units	100	n.a.
Tractor assembly	3	2,500 units	100	n.a.
Sewing machines	30	155,000 units	96 ⎫	0.4
Textile bobbins	11	115,000 gross	76 ⎭	
Domestic hardware	77	Rs.10 million	18	0.2
Utensils	87	6,710 tons	22	0.4
Refrigerators	2	10,000 units	100	n.a.
Dry cells	9	104 million units	92	n.a.
Storage batteries	9	187,000 units	80	n.a.
Electric bulbs	2	9.1 million units	100 ⎫	0.3
Fluorescent tubes	3	1.3 million units	100 ⎭	
Electric motors	21	580,000 h.p.	68 ⎫	
Switch gear	11	Rs.34 million	74 ⎬	1.2
Transformers	6	950,000 KVA	86 ⎭	
Fans	50	400,000 units	56	0.5
Radios	13	500,000 units	71 ⎫	1.6
Television	5	76,000 units	86 ⎭	
Bicycles	5	242,000 units	92	0.7
Motor vehicle assembly	5	13,900 units	86	n.a.
Shipbuilding and repairing	8	Rs.11.5 million	83	1.0
		Total		16.0

ᵃ Value added is included in vegetable ghee.

SOURCE: See text.

The concentration ratios are generally high. The simple average for the 82 industries is 70%. Only cotton textiles and its related industries, artificial silk textiles, wheat and rice milling, edible oils, hardware and utensils, paint, and tanning have concentration ratios below 33%. If we take 33% as the starting point for significant oligopoly formation,[8] over three-fifths of the manufacturing value added that could be measured originated in oligopolistic industries.[9] Alternatively, a composite figure for concentration could be achieved by weighting each industry's concentration ratio by its percentage contribution to total value added in manufacturing.[10] This weighted average four-firm concentration ratio comes to 51% for Pakistan.[11]

There are three factors that should be mentioned that qualify the use of these concentration ratios. First, the industrial concentration figures presented here, unfortunately, neglect unreported production and producers. In

[8] Scherer uses 40% as the point at which "oligopoly is beginning to rear its head" in American industry but, as I shall argue in Chapter 7, the Pakistani institutional context calls for a lower starting point. See Scherer, *op.cit.*, p. 60.

[9] Industries in Tables 5-1 and 5-2 with 33% concentration or over accounted for 46.6% of value added. Since the two tables together cover 74.3% of value added in Pakistan, the first figure represents 62.7% of the value added covered in Tables 5-1 and 5-2.

[10] In this case, it is the industry's contribution to the total of value added covered in Tables 5-1 and 5-2.

[11] This average industrial concentration, weighted by value added, should not be confused with the overall concentration figures presented in Chapter 4. The use of value added weights for the individual industry concentration ratios permits the construction of an average concentration figure that takes into account the relative importance of the various industries.

many traditional consumer good industries, small cottage producers are usually unregistered and unreported but may provide a significant alternative source of supply for consumers. Hand-loom weaving, leather goods, very small wheat and rice mills, and "gur" (an unrefined brown sugar) production are probably the most important of these. But Smith found that even in an industry as "modern" and producer-goods-oriented as diesel engine production, there were a significant number of unregistered firms.[12] To the extent that the outputs of these unregistered firms in the various industries are good substitutes for the outputs of the registered firms, the reported concentration ratios are overstatements of the true ratios.

Second, the implications of these concentration figures for market behavior and performance were strongly influenced by the existence of competing imports. These imports, however, were almost always subject to quotas or high tariffs, so they were far less than a perfect check on the behavior of domestic firms with market power. This point will receive a more complete discussion in Chapters 6 and 7.

Finally, to the extent that high transport costs created local monopolies, the national concentration figures understate the real concentration in local markets. However, particularly in West Pakistan the rail and road transportation network was well developed, and transport costs probably did not create significant marketing barriers in most areas. This last proposition can be subjected to a crude test, by making rough comparisons of railroad transport costs in Pakistan to those in the United States.

[12] Edward H. Smith, "The Diesel Engine Industry of Daska, Sialkot District," Mimeo, U.S. AID Mission to Pakistan (Rawalpindi, 1969).

The latter is used as a base, because data are readily available and because the U.S. is considered to have a system of relatively cheap transport.

The relevant figures for a comparison are the freight costs in each country relative to domestic prices in that country. Accordingly, I have expressed the average freight costs for 100 ton-miles in each country as a percentage of the domestic wholesale prices of a number of similar manufactured items in each country.[13] These figures are shown in Table 5-3. These are very rough figures, since in reality each item in each country had its own freight rate that was different from the average rates used in the table. But the differences are probably in the same directions in both countries. Value-of-service rate making is as prevalent in Pakistan as it is in the United States. From the table, it appears that ton-mile freight costs were generally a smaller percentage of wholesale prices in West Pakistan than in the U.S. In only 2 of the 16 items were U.S. average freight costs lower as a percentage of the wholesale price. In East Pakistan the picture is more mixed; U.S. relative freight costs were lower than those in East Pakistan for about two-thirds of the items.[14]

In West Pakistan, then, transport costs probably did not create marketing barriers that were any greater than those found in an industrialized country with a good transportation network. In East Pakistan, however, higher transport costs may have generated greater marketing barriers.

[13] The choice of items was determined entirely by the availability of comparable items and comparable prices in the wholesale price index "baskets" of both countries.

[14] These comparisons ignore the actual distance that commodities actually had to travel, but there is no readily available way of determining these.

TABLE 5-3
Comparative Wholesale Prices and Freight Costs, Pakistan and the United States, August 1967

Item	Wholesale Price		Average Freight Charge for 100 Ton-Miles as a % of Wholesale Price per Ton		
	Pakistan	U.S.	West Pakistan	East Pakistan	U.S.
Cotton yarn	Rs.22.50-23.33/ 10 lbs.	$0.565/lb.	0.14-0.15%	0.32-35%	0.12%
Grey cotton cloth	Rs.1.47-1.95/yd.	$0.183-0.245/yd.	3.46-4.59[a]	8.00-10.61[a]	5.35-7.16[a]
Coke	Rs.212.23-266.00/ton	$33.00-34.50/ton	2.54-3.18	5.87-7.35	3.79-3.97
Gasoline	Rs.3.83/Imp. gal.	$0.120-0.128/gal.	2.20[b]	5.08[b]	10.23-10.92[b]
Kerosene	Rs.11.52-13.54/ 8 Imp. gal.	$0.105-0.112/gal.	4.99-5.86[b]	11.53-13.54[b]	11.67-12.47[b]
Diesel oil	Rs.1.32-1.42/Imp. gal.	$0.088-090/gal.	5.94-6.39[b]	13.73-14.77[b]	14.55-14.87[b]
Soda ash	Rs.49.00/100 lbs.	$1.55/100 lbs.	0.69	1.59	4.23
Caustic soda	Rs.64.37/100 lbs.	$3.10/100 lbs.	0.52	1.20	2.11
Acetic acid	Rs.1.75/lb.	$0.14/lb.	0.19	0.44	0.47
Stearic acid	Rs.1.62/lb.	$0.183/lb.	0.21	0.49	0.36

TABLE 5-3 (*Continued*)

Item	Wholesale Price		Average Freight Charge for 100 Ton-Miles as a % of Wholesale Price per Ton		
	Pakistan	U.S.	West Pakistan	East Pakistan	U.S.
Zinc Oxide	Rs.177.50/100 lb.	$0.153/lb.	0.19	0.44	0.43
Soap	Rs.6.60/66 oz.	$0.405/lb.	0.21	0.49	0.16
Pig iron	Rs.594.37/ton	$59.60-63.667/ton	1.14	2.63	2.06-2.20
Steel bars	Rs.1425.00/ton	$11.154/100 lbs.	0.47	1.09	0.59
Cement	Rs.128-169.50/ton	$3,407/376 lbs.	3.98-5.27	9.20-12.18	7.23
Cigarettes	Rs.22.50-32.40/1,000	$5.065-5.261/1,000	0.21-0.30[c]	0.49-0.69[c]	0.25-0.26[c]

Average freight cost per ton-mile:
West Pakistan: Rs.0.0675 (1967-1968)
East Pakistan: Rs.0.1560 (1967-1968)
United States: $.0131 (1967)

[a] Average freight cost per 100 ton-miles per yard of cloth.
[b] Average freight cost per 100 ton-miles per U.S. gallon.
[c] Average freight cost per 100 ton-miles per 1000 cigarettes.

SOURCES: Government of Pakistan, Central Statistical Office, *Monthly Statistical Bulletin* (October 1968); U.S. Department of Labor, Bureau of Labor Statistics, *Wholesale Prices and Price Indexes* (August 1967).

Overall, these three qualifications probably do not affect the basic industrial concentration picture significantly. Average concentration was high in Pakistan; concentrated oligopoly was definitely the most common pattern.

A comparison of Pakistan's concentration by industry with that of other countries is yet more difficult than comparisons of overall concentration. In addition to differences in coverage, concepts, and weightings across countries that hamper any attempts, there are also differences in the definitions of industries. The efforts of Adelman, Bain, and Pryor at international comparisons are testimonials to these difficulties.[15] Consequently, I prefer to restrict the comparison to that of Pakistan with the United States, since I am familiar with the statistical base of the latter.[16] Table 5-4 presents the four-firm concentration ratio for Pakistan and for the United States for

[15] Morris A. Adelman, "Monopoly and Concentration: Comparisons in Time and Space," *Revista Internazionale di Scienze Economiche e Commerciali* (August 1965); Joe S. Bain, *International Differences in Industrial Structure* (New Haven, 1966); and Frederick L. Pryor, "An International Comparison of Concentration Ratios," *Review of Economics and Statistics* (May 1972).

[16] Phlips' study opened up the possibility of comparisons with France, Italy, the Netherlands, and Belgium, but I could only find 16 industries that were comparable between these countries and Pakistan. Further, Phlips' concentration ratios are based on employment. To the extent that the larger firms in an industry are more capital-intensive and less labor-intensive, this would give the figures from Phlips' study a serious downward bias compared to the Pakistan figures. See Louis Phlips, *Effects of Industrial Concentration: A Cross-Section Analysis for the Common Market* (Amsterdam, 1971).

TABLE 5-4

Concentration by Industry, Pakistan and the United States, 1967-1968

	Pakistan	United States[a]
Cotton textiles	25%	30%
Knitting	10	15
Dying, bleaching and finishing	10	42
Jute textiles	37	70
Wool textiles	48	51
Artificial silk textiles	10	46
Rayon yarn	100	89
Nylon yarn	100	91
Cigarettes	92	81
Vegetable ghee	45	42
Paper	100	26
Paperboard	88	24
Caustic soda	100	51
Sulfuric acid	100	54
Tires and tubes	97	71
Cement	86	28
Fertilizer	100	33
Petroleum refinery	100	32
West Pakistan		
Rice milling	12	45
Wheat and grain milling	14	37
Shoes	41	27
Tanning	30	20
Artificial leather cloth	63	33
Carpets	33	26
Paint	30	23
Ink	56	46
Soap and detergents	36	64
Cosmetics	46	36
Toothpaste	74	75
Distilleries	82	52
Glycerine	91	71
Carbon dioxide	91	73
Acetylene	100	80
Ferrous wire	87	24
Non-ferrous wire	87	38
Nails	43	34
Screws	80	17

TABLE 5-4 (*Continued*)

Concentration by Industry, Pakistan and the United States, 1967-1968

	West Pakistan	United States[a]
Metal cans	35	70
Sewing machines	96	80
Domestic hardware	18	15
Utensils	22	60
Dry cell batteries	92	85
Storage batteries	80	61
Electric bulbs	100	88
Electric motors	68	44
Switch gear	74	52
Transformers	86	64
Fans	56	47
Radios	71	48
Television	86	64
Shipbuilding	83	42
Unweighted Average	66	49

[a] Based on value of shipments.

SOURCES: Tables 5-1 and 5-2; U.S. Department of Commerce, Bureau of the Census, *1967 Census of Manufacturers*, Concentration Ratios in Manufacturing, Parts 1 and 2 (Washington, D.C., 1970 and 1971).

51 industries of comparable scope.[17] (The U.S. figures are for 1967 and are measured on shipments.) The Pakistani ratios are generally higher. The simple average of the 51 industries is 66% for Pakistan and 49% for the U.S. Further, Scherer found that the weighted (by value added) average four-firm concentration ratio for all U.S. manufacturing in 1963 and 1966 was 39%.[18] The com-

[17] Some industries that are nominally the same are excluded. For example, motor vehicle assembly in Pakistan, which is purely the assembly of knocked-down vehicles from abroad, is very different from the American motor vehicle industry, which is fully integrated into the manufacture of many component parts.

[18] Scherer, *op.cit.*, p. 63.

parable figure from the samples in Tables 5-1 and 5-2 is 51%.

From these figures, I conclude that Pakistan's industrial structure is at least as concentrated as that of the United States and is probably somewhat more concentrated. It is only the heavy weight of the cotton textile industry, with its comparatively low concentration ratio, that keeps the Pakistan weighted average even close to that of the United States. Not much more, however, can be said.

Industrial Concentration Among the Leading Families

In addition to the four-firm concentration ratios presented above, we can also determine the share of these markets controlled by the 43 leading families and groups. Table 5-5 presents these figures, along with the position, if any, of these families among the four largest firms or organizations in each industry.

These families were the dominant forces in all textiles except artificial silk, in sugar, cement, some chemicals, petroleum refining, motor vehicle and tractor assembly, and light bulbs. If we weight the percentage control of an industry by the industry's contribution to manufacturing value added, 38% of the value added of the sample originated in the firms controlled by the 43 largest families and groups. This is remarkably consistent with the earlier finding that 42% of manufacturing assets were controlled by these groups. Further, if we count only those firms controlled by the leading families which were among the top four in each industry, we can account for two-thirds of the average (weighted by value added) four-firm concentration ratio by industry. Not too surprisingly, then, the leading families appear to have achieved their substantial control over all Pakistan in-

TABLE 5-5

Industrial Concentration by the Leading 43 Families and Groups, 1968

	Percentage of Industry Controlled by Largest 43 Families and Groups	Position of Families Among Largest Four Firms in Industry
A. ALL PAKISTAN		
Cotton spinning	51%	1st, 2nd, 3rd, 4th
Cotton weaving	57	1, 2, 3, 4
Jute textiles	53	1, 3, 4 (#2 is government-controlled)
Wool textiles	52	1, 2, 3
Artificial silk textiles	9	–
Rayon yarn	100	1, 2 (only 2 firms)
Nylon yarn	60	1, 2
Cigarettes	22	3 (#1, 2 are foreign-controlled)
Sugar	59	2, 3, 4 (#1 is government-controlled)
Vegetable ghee	33	1, 3 (#2 is foreign)
Tea blending	32	3, 4 (#1, 2 are foreign)
Paper and paperboard	55	2, 3, 4 (#1 is government)
Caustic soda	100	1, 2, 3 (only 3 firms)
Soda ash	–	–
Sulfuric acid	8	3 (only 3 firms, #1 is government)
Tires and tubes	–	–
Cement	47	3, 4 (#1, 2 are government)
Fertilizer	–	(only 3 firms; all are government or foreign)
Petroleum refining	60	1, 3 (#2 is government, #4 is foreign)

TABLE 5-5 (*Continued*)

	Percentage of Industry Controlled by Largest 43 Families and Groups	Position of Families Among Largest Four Firms in Industry
B. WEST PAKISTAN		
Rice milling	–	–
Wheat and grain milling	1	–
Solvent oil extraction	50	1, 2
Shoes	–	– (#1 is foreign)
Tanning	–	–
Artificial leather cloth	52	1, 4
Carpets	–	–
Canvas	–	–
Lubricating oils	47	3, 4 (#1, 2 are foreign)
Paint	6	4
Ink	27	1
Soap	7	4
Starch	–	–
Glucose	–	–
Ammonium chloride	–	– (only 1 firm)
Bleaching powder	100	1, 2 (only 2 firms)
Distilleries	87	1, 2, 3
Glycerine	11	4 (#1 is foreign)
Sulfur refining	–	–
Hydrochloric acid	96	1 (only 3 firms)
Formaldehyde	100	1 (only 1 firm)
Carbon dioxide	11	3
Oxygen	–	–
Acytelene	–	–
Steel foundry	20	1 (2, 3 are government)
Steel rerolling	27	1, 2
Conduit pipe	–	–
G.I. pipe	40	1
M.S. pipe	20	2

TABLE 5-5 (*Continued*)

	Percentage of Industry Controlled by Largest 43 Families and Groups	Position of Families Among Largest Four Firms in Industry
B. WEST PAKISTAN		
Ferrous wire	43	1
Non-ferrous wire	–	–
Barbed wire	12	4
Nails	–	–
Wood screws	–	–
Steel furniture	–	–
Metal cans	13	1
Razor blades	54	1
Tractor assembly	80	1, 2 (only 3 firms)
Sewing machines	–	–
Textile bobbins	–	– (#2 is foreign)
Domestic hardware	–	–
Utensils	–	–
Refrigerators	47	2 (only 2 firms)
Dry cell batteries	–	–
Storage batteries	–	–
Electric bulbs	73	1 (only 2 firms)
Fluorescent tubes	47	1 (only 3 firms)
Electric motors	28	1
Switch gear	–	– (#1, 2 are foreign-controlled)
Transformers	–	– (#3, 4 are foreign-controlled)
Fans	–	–
Radios	–	– (#3 is foreign)
Television	–	– (#4 is foreign)
Bicycles	41	1
Motor vehicle assembly	86	1, 2, 3, 4
Shipbulding and repairing	7	– (#1 is government)

SOURCE: See text.

dustry by achieving control over most of the leading firms in the leading industries.

Retailing

Finally, we turn our attention to market structure at the retailing level. Popular discussions in LDC's frequently allude to monopolistic elements and market power in retailing. Whenever retail prices in Pakistan rose—whether for seasonal reasons, because of temporary shortage of supplies, or because of general inflationary conditions—newspaper articles and editorials frequently blamed the rises on "greedy" retailers, "hoarders," "speculators," and "monopolistic elements" in retailing in general.[19] This chapter is the logical place to deal with these issues. Can one say anything about these claims?

First, there is nothing in the theory of the firm or the theory of monopoly that would lead to any conclusions about inflation or the raising of prices.[20] The theory is static; monopolies *maintain* high, profit-maximizing prices. They change their prices only if demand, supply, or cost conditions change, but so will a group of competitors.[21] On theoretical grounds, then, we can dismiss this line of argument.

[19] These charges also gave rise to suggestions that government-operated "fair price" shops be established to circumvent these monopolistic retailers.

[20] A further discussion of this point is found in George J. Stigler, "Administered Prices and Oligopolistic Inflation," *Journal of Business* (January 1962).

[21] One possible exception would be the following: if supply were perfectly elastic, a shift in demand that was accompanied by a change in the slope of the demand curve would cause the monopolist to change his price while a group of competitors

There is also some empirical evidence that can throw light on this point. The Central Statistical Organization conducted a number of censuses of establishments in Pakistani cities between 1962 and 1968. These cities are shown in the left-hand side of Table 5-6, along with their estimated population, the number of pharmacies per 100,000 population, and the number of food and general stores per 100,000 population. Rather than try to determine *a priori* what is or is not a competitive number of retailing outlets, I have tried to compare each city with a city in the United States of the same population, along with the latter's retailers. Few observers have complained about monopoly power at the retailing level in the United States. These figures are presented on the right-hand side of Table 5-6.

The comparison indicates that Pakistani cities are about as well provided with pharmacies as are comparable U.S. cities, and that they seem to have relatively greater numbers of other retailers. Pakistani retailers are, of course, smaller than their American counterparts, and they are stocked with a much smaller variety of goods, but it is their numbers that ought to determine their competitiveness. The numbers seem to indicate a competitive structure for retailing in the cities.

Over half of the Pakistani population, however, lived

---

would not. Thus, if demand became more inelastic, a monopolist would raise his price. This might explain some of the observed price behavior at the time of holidays and festivals, when demand tends to increase and probably also becomes more inelastic. Note that this effect could occur anywhere along the distribution chain and not necessarily at the retail level. Also, one would want to be confident that the goods in question were in elastic supply before accepting this explanation.

TABLE 5-6

Comparative Numbers of Retail Establishments, Pakistan and the U.S., 1962-1968

Pakistan City	Estimated Population[a]	Pharmacies per 100,000 Pop.	Food and General Stores per 100,000 Pop.	U.S. City	Estimated Population[b]	Pharmacies per 100,000 Pop.	"Other Retailers" per 100,000 Pop.[c]
Karachi, W. P.	2,151,400	11	403	St. Louis, Mo.	2,272,400	28	397
Lahore, W. P.	1,537,200	22	461	Cleveland, Ohio	2,049,500	24	364
Dacca, E. P.	900,800	40	740	Minneapolis, Minn.	1,619,800	22	345
Lyallpur, W. P.	602,300	10	363	Dallas, Tex.	1,362,600	25	485
Multan, W. P.	462,000	15	353	Portland, Ore.	916,200	22	406
Chittagong, E. P.	398,800	35	551	Tampa, Fla.	880,900	28	494
Peshawar, W. P.	254,500	43	589	Gary, Ind.	602,800	26	345
Gujranwala, W. P.	250,000	12	502	Honolulu, Hawaii	596,400	14	344
Khulna, E. P.	202,700	14	703	Fort Lauderdale, Fla.	466,000	29	566
Sukkur, W. P.	119,500	24	452	Tulsa, Okla.	441,400	30	513
				Fresno, Calif.	410,800	25	487
				Knoxville, Tenn.	395,200	27	407
				Erie, Pa.	256,000	20	464
				Austin, Tex.	254,000	28	416
				Santa Barbara, Calif.	251,300	25	474
				Lorain, Ohio	242,800	17	355
				McAllen, Tex.	203,800	23	474
				Raleigh, N. C.	201,600	23	387
				Lynchburg, Va.	121,600	24	451

TABLE 5-6 (Continued)

Pakistan City	Estimated Population[a]	Pharmacies per 100,000 Pop.	Food and General Stores per 100,000 Pop.	U.S. City	Estimated Population[b]	Pharmacies per 100,000 Pop.	"Other Retailers" per 100,000 Pop.[c]
Bahawalpur, W. P.	119,100	18	411	Pueblo, Colo.	119,000	23	376
Quetta, W. P.	117,900	25	750	Sioux City, Iowa	114,900	27	476
Mardan, W. P.	98,500	32	628	Boise, Idaho	100,700	27	511
Sahiwal, W. P.	95,800	22	475	Wilmington, N.C.	96,900	34	624
				Bloomington, Ill.	95,600	28	473
Barisal, E. P.	75,700	91	666	Sherman, Tex.	77,600	24	591
				Laredo, Tex.	75,600	24	495
Saidpur, E. P.	69,600	29	599	San Angelo, Tex.	73,600	31	490
Rajshahi, E. P.	68,200	31	723	Midland, Tex.	66,400	36	512
Average (unweighted)		28	551			26	433
Average excluding Barisal		24	544				

[a] Estimated population at the time of the relevant census of establishments.

[b] Estimated for 1966 for the standard metropolitan statistical area.

[c] Includes all retailers except drug stores, automotive dealers, gasoline service stations, eating and drinking places, and non-store retailers.

SOURCES: Government of Pakistan, Central Statistical Office, *Summary of Findings of the Census of Establishments in Selected Cities, 1962-1966* (Karachi, 1968); U.S. Department of Commerce, Bureau of the Census, *1967 Census of Business,* Retail Trade, Sales Size (Washington, D.C., 1970); U.S. Department of Commerce, Bureau of the Census, *Population Estimates and Projections,* Series P-25, No. 427 (Washington, D.C., 1969).

in rural areas, where retail outlets clearly were more sparse. Were they at the mercy of retailers with monopoly power? The answer is a probable yes, but this is true for the rural population of virtually all countries. Also, any major purchase of manufactured goods probably involved a trip to a larger Pakistani population center where more competition was available.

Chapter 6

The Origins of Concentration

THE findings of the two preceding chapters have indicated that the Pakistan economy experienced high rates of concentration for the 1960's, both across the entire manufacturing sector and for individual industries. This chapter examines the origins of both kinds of concentration. The analysis of Chapter 2 indicated that the establishment and maintenance of market power required the existence of significant barriers to entry. This chapter examines the role of scale economies barriers and scarce resources barriers in maintaining industrial concentration. It is also argued that scarce resources barriers, mostly created by deliberate government policy, were crucial to the continued domination of the manufacturing sector by the leading industrial families and groups.

It is worth emphasizing at the beginning that the connection between concentration and barriers to entry was not one way. Barriers created pockets of concentration and economic power. This economic power, in turn, generated political power that maintained these barriers or erected new ones. Both "Tariffs are the Mother of Trusts" and "Trusts are the Mother of Tariffs" have validity. In this sense, the contents of this chapter and the discussion of the effects of concentration in the following chapter are logically linked.

Economies of Scale Barriers

Unfortunately, little is known about the extent of economies of scale and the optimum size of firms in LDC's. Scale economies seem to be important in developed countries in industries like rayon, nylon, cement, fertilizer, petroleum refining, chemicals, and vehicle assembly. Bain, for example, cites figures indicating that, for the technology available in the United States in the early 1950's, the minimum efficient plant size for rayon production would have been five times as large as the total of Pakistani production in 1968.[1] Efficient automobile assembly in the United States requires a volume of 200,000 units a year, or 15 times the 1968 Pakistani capacity.[2]

These kinds of estimates, though, are for American technology that has been designed for American capital and labor costs. We simply do not know how well these translate to LDC, and specifically Pakistani, conditions. I strongly suspect that the minimum efficient scales would be lower if the technologies were twisted in a labor-intensive direction, but it is difficult to tell how much of a difference this would make. It probably would not make much difference in areas like cement, fertilizer, and petroleum refining. In other areas, though, like sugar, vegetable ghee (shortening), and tea blending, labor-intensive technologies would probably create appreciably lower efficient scales than prevailing Western technologies. Since, though, the technology that has been installed in Pakistani industry has tended to be capital-intensive, we can only say that economies of scale have been more

[1] Joe S. Bain, *Barriers to New Competition* (Cambridge, Mass., 1956), pp. 241-243.

[2] Lawrence J. White, *The Automobile Industry since 1945* (Cambridge, Mass., 1971), Ch. 4.

important than they might have been if more labor-intensive methods had been encouraged.[3]

But economies of scale cannot explain all of the industrial concentration found in Pakistan. A cotton textile spinning mill of 25,000 spindles is generally considered to be the minimum efficient size for Pakistani circumstances. If Pakistan's spinning capacity were divided among equal-sized firms, 112 firms could be in the industry, and the four-firm concentration ratio would be below 4%. The 4 leading families in fact controlled 20% of the spindles in the industry, while two-thirds of the factories in the industry were below minimum efficient size. We have to look to another kind of barrier to entry to explain these phenomena.

Scarce Resource Barriers: Foreign Exchange Licensing

The ability of an entrepreneur to enter an industry and the scale at which he could enter was determined by his ability to get investment licenses and the licenses to import capital goods from abroad. Once established, he needed further licenses for his supply of imported raw materials and spare parts. These did indeed constitute scarce resources barriers, and the structure of industries was largely shaped by the granting of these licenses.

[3] Low duties on capital goods imports, low interest loans to buy capital goods, rapid depreciation allowances, technical assistance from Western technicians who are accustomed to thinking in capital-intensive terms, and tied project aid, which is at least partly designed to aid the capital goods producers of the donor countries, are among the reasons for the bias toward capital-intensity. On the evidence concerning the capital-intensiveness of Pakistani industry, see Azizur Rahman Kahn, "Capital-Intensity and the Efficiency of Factor Use: A Comparative Study of the Observed Capital-Labour Ratios of Pakistani Industries," *Pakistan Development Review* (Summer 1970).

Further, these barriers contributed significantly to the continued industrial dominance of the 43 leading families and groups. Since virtually all industrial investment required imported capital goods, the licensing of imported capital goods was the effective investment licensing, and thus we shall concentrate on import licensing as the crucial scarce resource barriers.

Pakistan's foreign exchange control system was extremely complex and often seemed to defy efforts to explain it completely.[4] The government's *Manual of Imports and Exports Control* was 440 pages long! From 1955 until 1972, Pakistan maintained an official exchange rate of Rs.4.76 = $1.00. A cascaded import tariff structure was imposed on this exchange rate: low duties for capital goods, moderate duties for raw materials, and high duties on consumer goods, with outright bans on some items. These duties were not raised high enough to restrict the demand for imports to the supply of foreign exchange at the going exchange rate, and thus the supply of foreign exchange had to be rationed administratively through licensing schemes.

There were three main licensing regimes. First, capital goods imports were under the control of the Pakistan Industrial Credit and Investment Corporation (PICIC), the Industrial Development Bank of Pakistan (IDBP),

---

[4] See S. N. H. Naqvi, "Import Licensing in Pakistan," *Pakistan Development Review* (Spring 1964); Philip S. Thomas, "Import Licensing and Import Liberalization in Pakistan," *Pakistan Development Review* (Winter 1966); Frank C. Child, "Liberalization of the Foreign Exchange Market," *Pakistan Development Review* (Summer 1968); Frank C. Child, "Reform of a Trade and Payments System: The Case of Pakistan," *Economic Development and Cultural Change* (July 1968); Bruce Glassburner, "Aspects of the Problem of Foreign Exchange Pricing in Pakistan," *Economic Development and Cultural Change* (July 1968).

and the Department of Industrial Promotion and Supplies (IP&S). These three bodies (plus, to a limited extent, the provincial governments of East and West Pakistan) were "sanctioning" agencies. They had the power to sanction an industrial project, which meant that they approved the release of foreign exchange for the necessary capital goods imports and they provided the financing for the project. The foreign exchange was usually from aid sources, and any domestic rupee financing came from Central Government sources.

Licensing of raw materials was through the Chief Controller of Imports and Exports (CCI&E). Raw material imports were allocated primarily on the basis of installed capacity. A firm's capacity would be assessed, and it would then receive an "entitlement." Each six months the CCI&E would determine the fraction of their entitlements that firms would be permitted to import; commercial importers, who could resell their goods, were also given allotments. The source of this foreign exchange was a mixture of program aid and Pakistan's own earned foreign exchange.

Finally, consumer goods imports were also licensed by the CCI&E. The attempt here was to strike a balance between demand, domestic supply of the goods, and available foreign exchange.

After January 1, 1959, a bonus voucher system overlay the system described above. Most manufactured exports earned bonus vouchers in addition to the Rs.4.76 per dollar. The bonus vouchers were earned at the rate of 20%-40% of the value of exports. Thus, the exporter of Rs.100 of manufactured exports also received Rs.20-Rs.40 in face value of bonus vouchers. These vouchers could be used to buy unlimited quantities of imports that were on a special bonus voucher list; i.e., these imports were not subject to licensing restrictions. The importer was required to present Rs.4.76 in face value bonus vouchers, in addition to Rs.4.76 in cash, for each dollar. Initially, the bonus import list and the licensed import list were not overlapping, but by the late 1960's items that were licensed could also be bought with bonus vouchers over and above the licensing system.[5]

These bonus vouchers could be sold by the original exporter to someone else who could use them for imports, and an organized market in bonus vouchers was organized on the Karachi Stock Exchange. The price of the vouchers fluctuated with supply and demand, but the price tended to remain within a range of 160%-180% of face value; i.e., an exporter who earned Rs.20 in face value bonus vouchers could sell them for Rs.32-Rs.36. By the same token, an importer wishing to buy $100 in imports using bonus vouchers was required to pay the Rs.476 for the foreign exchange plus Rs.762-Rs.857 for the Rs.476 face value bonus vouchers.

As the exchange position of Pakistan worsened in the late 1960's, increasing numbers of consumer goods and some raw materials were importable with bonus vouchers only. After 1967, bonus vouchers were required for many raw materials imports, but only at a 50% rate ("cash-cum-bonus"). These raw materials, though, were still subject to licensing.

The bonus vouchers represented a partial and non-uniform devaluation of the rupee. They also represented a safety valve on the licensing system. But for the importer without a license, they were an expensive safety valve, for he had to pay over two and one-half times as much for his imports as the importer who had a license

[5] For a year, though, in 1967 even bonus imports became subject to licensing restrictions, but this was subsequently dropped.

at the official exchange rate. In the case of capital goods, they were not a complete circumvention of the licensing system, since even with bonus vouchers a purchaser of imported capital goods needed the approval of the IP&S.

Finally, exporters of manufactured goods, in addition to their bonus voucher receipts, had special access to imported inputs that circumvented the normal licensing procedures.

This very brief description of the import licensing regimes indicates the complicated system that could protect firms lucky enough to get within it and that acted as a barrier to firms outside. The firm that could get a sanction from PICIC, IDBP, or IP&S was able to get its capital goods at the official exchange rate and it received automatic financing on very favorable terms. On the basis of its installed capacity it became eligible for raw materials and spare parts imports. If it was producing consumer goods for the domestic market, it had the benefit of an extra barrier at the marketing stage: high protective tariffs, restrictively licensed competitive imports, and import bans. If it was producing for the export market, it received bonus vouchers and favorable access to imports. By contrast, the firm that could not get a sanction had to buy its capital equipment second-hand or at a substantial mark-up (reflecting the scarcity premium of the foreign exchange) from a commercial importer.[6] It did not have automatic financing available to it. Since its capacity was not sanctioned, the firm would have a great deal more difficulty receiving an import entitlement; in the absence of an entitlement, it had to buy its imported raw materials and spare parts from commercial im-

[6] See Mohiuddin Alamgir, "The Domestic Prices of Imported Commodities in Pakistan: A Further Study," *Pakistan Development Review* (Spring 1968).

porters, again paying the scarcity value of the foreign exchange.

The extent of this protection has been documented by Lewis and Guisinger.[7] Taking into account the tariffs on inputs, the tariffs on outputs, and the scarcity mark-up permitted by the restrictive licensing of competitive imports, they found that the median industry of a sample of 32 industries received 78.5% of its value added from the overall protection system in 1963-1964; for consumer goods alone, the median industry received 87% of its value added from protection. Nine of the 32 industries were wholly dependent on protection for their value added.[8] The extra value added permitted by this protection was, of course, shared between labor and capital. But, as we saw earlier, capital's average share of value added was over 70%, and it is most likely that its marginal share of the value added permitted by protection was at least that high.

The disadvantage experienced by a firm that was outside the licensing system has also been documented by Lewis and Guisinger.[9] They found that access to direct import licensing privileges generated 39% extra value added for firms with the licenses over the value added of

[7] Stephen R. Lewis and Stephen E. Guisinger, "Measuring Protection in a Developing Country: The Case of Pakistan," *Journal of Political Economy* (December 1968).

[8] This need not mean that there was actual physical waste in the use of inputs, only that the system of protection had skewed production processes so that at world prices the industries would have generated zero or negative value added. For a further discussion of this point, see Stephen E. Guisinger, "Negative Value Added and the Theory of Effective Protection," *Quarterly Journal of Economics* (August 1969).

[9] Stephen R. Lewis and Stephen E. Guisinger, "The Structure of Protection in Pakistan," in *The Structure of Protection in Developing Countries*, Bela Balassa, ed. (Baltimore, 1971).

firms without licenses.[10] Small wonder, then, that entrepreneurs who were within the licensing system, despite
their claimed ideological commitments to a "free enterprise system," were the most ardent supporters of the
licensing system. It is not surprising, either, that there
was substantial excess demand for investment sanctions.
A sanction to invest in a textile mill, even an inefficiently
small unit, was a highly sought prize. In 1968, for example, PICIC received applications for Rs.1,319 million
in loans, whereas it granted only Rs.383 million in loans
that year.[11] Since sanctions were clearly not available to
all comers, they did in fact constitute a substantial barrier
to entry.

Licensing and the Leading Families

The dominant position of the leading industrial families and groups was related to their mastery of the licensing system. This had to be true, since one could become
a big manufacturer only by using imported capital equipment, and one could obtain the imported capital equipment only by getting an investment sanction. As one
became big, one became a likely recipient of future licenses.

The relationship between the important industrial families and groups and the licensing system can be documented to some extent. The government of Pakistan
published a directory of the industrial units sanctioned
by the various sanctioning agencies during the Second
Five-Year Plan (1960-1965).[12] Not all of the sanctions

[10] Stephen R. Lewis, *Pakistan: Industrialization and Trade
Policies* (London, 1970), p. 94.

[11] Pakistan Industrial Credit and Investment Corporation, *11th
Annual Report* (Karachi, 1969).

[12] Government of Pakistan, Department of Investment, Pro-

were actually used, but the list provides a good measurement of the intentions of the licensing agencies. Over these five years, these agencies issued licenses for Rs.2,968 million in imported capital goods to non-government companies. A compilation of the value of the licenses issued to the companies controlled by the 43 largest families and groups indicates that these families received capital goods licenses worth Rs.1,512 million, or 50.9% of the total. This is a figure that is quite close to the 51.5% figure in Table 4-7 for the control of these families over private (non-government) manufacturing assets. The leading families' dominant position in manufacturing was indeed related to their mastery of the licensing system.

We can make a further test of the connection between licensing and the dominant families and groups. The 1968 assets of each of the leading families were regressed against the foreign exchange licenses it received between 1960 and 1965. This is a rough test, since some of the licenses were never used or the capital equipment might have been imported after 1968 or some of the leading families might have acquired most of their investment sanctions before 1960 or after 1965. Still, a significant result was obtained, as follows (the numbers in parentheses are t-statistics):

(1) $A = 75.17 + 1.95\ FEL$
      (3.80)   (5.62)

$$R^2 = 0.43$$
43 Observations

where A is the 1968 assets (in millions of rupees) controlled by a family (average: Rs.140.0 million) and FEL

___

motion, and Supplies, *Directory of Industrial Units Sanctioned During Second Five Year Plan Period (1960-65)* (Karachi, 1967).

is the foreign exchange licenses received (in millions of rupees) by the family (average: Rs.35.3 million).

Equation (1) indicates that there was a strong and significant relationship between family importance in 1968 and the receipt of foreign exchange licenses for capital goods in the 1960-1965 period. But we need to know what determined the distribution of the licenses. Were they distributed in a way to maintain or increase concentration? Were they distributed in a way that was significantly different from the pattern of capital goods imports that would have occurred in the absence of licensing? This last question is very difficult to answer. But one could argue that the pattern of capital goods imports in the absence of licensing would be related to the profitability of firms, since the more profitable firms would find it worthwhile to expand their operations. The pattern of profitability would, of course, be somewhat different in the absence of licensing than in its presence. Still, the distribution of licenses seems to have been unrelated either to the reported profitability of family-controlled firms at the beginning of the licensing period or to the resultant profitability that accrued from the licenses. This is shown in equations (2) and (3) for the 24 families that controlled companies publicly listed in 1961[13] (the numbers in parentheses are t-statistics):

(2) $FELP = 23.03 + 987.01 \, \pi61$
           (1.16)   (0.01)

$$R^2 = 0.04$$

(3) $FELP = 47.71 - 470.45 \, \pi68$
           (2.83)   (0.54)

$$R^2 = 0.01$$

[13] Since the set of foreign exchange licenses discussed here were first issued only in November 1960, the fiscal year 1961 was, for most firms, prior to their receipt of licenses.

where *FELP* is the foreign exchange licenses for publicly listed firms only (average: Rs.40.28 million), $\pi 61$ is the reported net profits on net worth of publicly listed holdings of these families in 1961 (average: 17%), and $\pi 68$ is the reported net profits on net worth of publicly listed holdings of these families in 1968 (average: 16%). The relationships are insignificant and in equation (3) the sign on the profitability term goes the wrong way.

Further, the pattern of capital goods licenses seems to have been related to the importance of a family at the beginning of the licensing period. If, by contrast, the licenses had been distributed randomly, we would still expect to find the relationship in equation (1), but we would not find any relationship with family size at the beginning of the period. This is seen in equation (4), where the licenses received by a family are regressed against the assets of publicly listed companies controlled by a family in 1961:

$$(4) \quad FELP = 10.77 + 0.52\,PA61$$
$$(0.99)\ (3.79)$$
$$R^2 = 0.40$$

where *PA61* are the assets of publicly listed firms controlled by a family in 1961 (average: Rs.56.80 million). Equation (4) indicates that, at the margin, an extra Rs.100 in assets for a family in 1961 meant an extra Rs.52 in capital goods licenses. The explanatory power of equation (4) is just about the same as the explanatory power of licenses on the publicly listed assets of these same 24 families in 1968, as is seen in equation (5):

$$(5) \quad PA68 = 89.47 + 2.32\,FELP$$
$$(2.61)\ (4.14)$$
$$R^2 = 0.44$$

where *PA68* is the assets of publicly listed firms controlled by a family in 1968 (average: Rs.182.8 million).
Thus, the asset size of a family near the beginning of the
licensing period is as closely correlated with the licenses
received as the asset size at the end of the period.

There is one further piece of evidence that can be
marshalled to support the argument that the wealth and
prestige of the large industrial families was influential
in their receipt of capital goods import licenses. The
Pakistan Industrial Credit and Investment Corporation
(PICIC) was the agency responsible for sanctioning
large-scale industrial projects. Between its inception in
1957 and the end of 1968, it sanctioned Rs.1,657 million
in loans and guarantees for industrial projects. During
the Second Plan (1960-1965), it sanctioned a third of
the private investment projects. There were 21 men
on the board of directors of PICIC in the 1960's. Five
were non-Pakistanis, representing the donor countries
and institutions who made the foreign exchange available
to PICIC for relending to private Pakistani companies.
Three were representatives of the Central, West, and
East Pakistan governments. The remaining 13 were Pakistanis from private life. Seven of these were members of
the leading industrial families: Adamjee, Bashir, Dawood, Fancy, Jalil, Rangoonwala, and Valika. The
Chairman of the Board was Mr. A. W. Adamjee. Though
the 43 leading industrial families and groups received
51% of the total investment sanctions in the Second Plan
period, they managed to receive 64% of the sanctions
distributed by PICIC between 1960 and 1965. The firms
controlled by the 7 families represented on the board of
directors received 21% of the PICIC sanctions, worth
Rs.208 million in foreign exchange. Only in May 1970
did the Central Government require PICIC to obtain

prior approval from the Central Government before sanctioning a project of a company controlled by a director of PICIC.

Undoubtedly, in the 1950's the industrial families became large because they received capital goods licenses at the time. The reasons why they in particular received the licenses must have been a combination of ability, initiative, influence, and luck. Unfortunately, data is not available to make a more precise determination. By the beginning of the 1960's, however, the industrial families were already large and influential. Their size and influence guaranteed that they would continue to receive the lion's share of the licenses, and their continued receipt of the licenses guaranteed that they would continue to dominate the industrial structure of Pakistan.

There was another source of financial support for the large industrial families and groups. The West Pakistan and East Pakistan Industrial Development Corporations were autonomous government agencies, authorized to establish and operate industrial projects and to aid the establishment and operation of private industrial projects. Official government policy was to encourage WPIDC and EPIDC to divest profitable projects to the private sector after they were established, though this was not a mandatory rule.

As of 1968, WPIDC had divested or aided 17 projects in which it no longer retained a strong voice. These had originally cost Rs.130 million, but their actual capital value in 1968 was probably closer to Rs.400 million. Eight of these projects, accounting for 80% of the original capital cost, were controlled by families included among the largest 43. EPIDC had divested or aided 33 projects with an original capital cost of Rs.710 million. Eleven were controlled by families among the largest 43, and these 11 accounted for 40% of the original capital cost.

Assistance to private undertakings meant that WPIDC and EPIDC provided equity and loan capital on favorable terms. Divestiture involved "protracted negotiations with private parties after which the offers [had] to be submitted before the Disinvestment Committee formed by the Government for taking final decision."[14] Did these organizations drive the hardest bargains they could? Might auctions have produced a better selling price for their divested assets? How were the particular projects and entrepreneurs chosen to whom assistance was given? Without complete knowledge of the alternatives, it is difficult to make any definitive statements. But it is difficult to believe that the dominant positions of the large industrial families did not influence the divestiture and assistance decision.

[14] West Pakistan Industrial Development Corporation, *Annual Report, 1967-68* (Karachi, 1969), p. 8.

Chapter 7

The Effects of Concentration

PAKISTAN is characterized by a high degree of overall concentration in its manufacturing sector and generally by oligopolies in its individual manufacturing markets. Chapter 2 indicated the general consequences that one might expect from these structural characteristics. This chapter discusses the effects—economic and non-economic—actually found in Pakistan. First, some institutional qualifications to the oligopoly structure found in Pakistan are discussed. Then, a simple model explaining industrial profit rates is presented. Innovation is mentioned. The economic performance of family and non-family firms is analyzed. The political influence and power that grew from and reinforced the economic power of the leading families is detailed. The chapter concludes with a discussion of the links between the skewed income distribution, taxation, and the public development effort in Pakistan.

Some Qualifications to the Oligopoly Structure

The findings of Chapter 5 indicated a widespread pattern of oligopoly markets in manufacturing. The more easily the members of an oligopoly can coordinate their actions, the more closely their performance in the market will approximate that of a monopoly. There were four structural aspects of the manufacturing markets in Pakistan that affected the ability of firms to coordinate their actions and act like monopolists.

First, government-controlled firms were dominant in a few industries. Over 80% of the fertilizer, over half of the cement, 38% of paper, a third of the sugar (90% of East Pakistan's production), and 10% of jute textiles were produced by government-controlled companies. Concentration in these markets, then, did not mean the creation of private power and wealth. But these government-controlled firms do not appear to have been competitive checks on the remaining private firms in these markets. The government-controlled firms were under pressure to show sizable profits, if not maximize them, and they were as vocal as private firms in asking for protection from imports and for favorable exchange rates on imported inputs. They were not noted for their aggressive competitiveness. Though the government-controlled firms were frequently accused of inefficiency, these accusations were usually aimed at alleged excessive labor hiring, inefficient use of other inputs, and politically inspired factory location choices; they were not based on any grounds that might be related to unhappiness over aggressive competitive behavior.

Second, open collusion, price-fixing, and other anticompetitive acts were not forbidden by Pakistani law. This made it easier for firms, even in low concentration industries, to coordinate their actions through trade associations. In a number of instances the Central Government encouraged coordinated price fixing, in the hope that this would keep prices low and stable; it rarely did. Also, there were no laws forbidding interlocking directorates within the same industry. Families who controlled a firm in an industry sometimes had family members on the boards of directors of competing firms in the same industry. Of the total of 249 corporate interlocks among family and non-family firms found in Chapter 4, 50 involved such instances. An additional 21 interlocks involved a family having members sitting on the boards of 2 competing firms in an industry, even though the family itself was not directly involved in that industry. Again, these kinds of interlocking directorates made coordination among competing firms easier.

Further, members of an industry were frequently dependent for their imported raw materials on one or a few importers, who could use their control over these inputs to monopolize and control the industry. Perhaps the clearest example of this was in the vegetable ghee (shortening) industry. All of the imported edible oil for this industry had to pass through the Liberty-American Tank Terminal Company in Karachi Port. The company was owned by Mr. M. A. Rangoonwala, who was also the largest manufacturer of vegetable ghee. This control over the entire supply of imported edible oil increased Mr. Rangoonwala's importance and power beyond just the size of his physical asset holdings. It may have been one of the reasons why he was on nine company boards of directors (see Table 4-15), despite his rank of only thirty-first by size of assets.

Third, the dependence of most industries on imported raw materials and spare parts and the restrictive licensing of those inputs put a damper on the ability of firms to compete with one another. It would make sense for a firm to try to compete with a rival by cutting its price only if it could expand production to meet the anticipated extra demand at the lower price. But if inputs, capital goods, and spare parts were stringently rationed, firms could not expand their outputs, and they would not bother to engage in price competition. The licensing of imported inputs effectively helped cartelize industries.

Fourth, domestic production in many markets was heavily supplemented by imports. For example, in 1968 the 2 Pakistani producers of rayon fiber produced 9 million pounds of rayon, but another 5.6 million pounds was imported. Table 7-1 gives the imports, as a percentage of domestic production, for a number of industries in 1967-1968.[1] Because of the difficulty of matching import classifications with domestic production classifications, a number of industries had to be excluded. Also, the broad categories in the table surely overestimate the extent to which imports were competing with domestic production. Rubber tires of some sizes may have been imported while other sizes were produced domestically, etc. The table indicates that imports were relatively unimportant in consumer goods industries, more important in intermediate goods industries, and generally quite important in capital goods industries.

If imported goods had been freely importable at zero or low rates of duty, these imports would have been an important constraint on the ability of domestic producers to exploit their market power. In effect, the barriers to entry at the marketing stage would have been low; transport costs and tariffs would have represented the only barriers. If domestic producers had tried to raise their prices above CIF import prices plus tariffs for any extended period of time, one would have seen imported products flooding the market until prices descended again.

But import duties on many items, particularly consumer goods, were not modest, as is seen in Table 7-2. Further, imports were generally licensed and could not be freely imported. Some categories of imports, though,

[1] The percentages were computed on the basis of CIF imports compared to the sum of imports and the value of domestic production less indirect taxes.

TABLE 7-1

Imports, as a Percentage of Total Supply, 1967-1968

Sugar	1%
Vegetable ghee	0
Manufactured tobacco	0
Cotton woven fabric	0
Furniture	8
Paper and paperboard	16
Articles of paper	13
Rubber products	37
Rayon yarn	38
Inorganic chemicals	32
Dyes	87
Paints and varnishes	24
Pharmaceutical products	17
Cosmetics	2
Soaps	4
Fertilizer	59
Leather and articles of leather	0
Footwear	0
Petroleum products	17
Glass and glass products	34
Cement	8
Structural clay products	54
Pottery	30
Iron and steel basic forms	32
Structural metal products	84
Cutlery	9
Heating, plumbing, and lighting equipment	20
Hand tools and hardware	68
Nuts and bolts	37
Engines and turbines	82
Agricultural machinery	78
Textile machinery	92
Metalworking machinery	95
Motors, generators, transformers, etc.	74
Communications equipment	37

SOURCES: Government of East Pakistan, *Census of Manufacturing Industries in East Pakistan, 1967-68*, mimeo (Dacca, 1971); Government of Punjab, *Census of Manufacturing Industries of West Pakistan, 1967-68*, mimeo (Lahore, 1970); Government of Pakistan, Central Statistical Office, *Monthly Statistical Bulletin* (October 1968).

TABLE 7-2

Average Rates of Import Duties

	1955-1956	1960-1961	1965-1966	1968-1969
Consumption goods:				
Essentials	35	55	70	70
Semi-luxuries	54	111	148	150
Luxuries	99	140	180	n.a.
Raw materials for consumption goods:				
Unprocessed	26	27	39 }	60
Processed	43	50	81 }	
Raw materials for capital goods:				
Unprocessed	23	28	40 }	66
Processed	38	40	69 }	
Capital goods:				
Consumer durables	71	85	114	n.a.
Machinery and equipment	14	17	34	34

SOURCES: G. M. Radhu, "The Rate Structure of Indirect Taxes in Pakistan," *Pakistan Development Review* (Autumn 1964); Philip S. Thomas, "Import Licensing and Import Liberalization in Pakistan," *Pakistan Development Review* (Winter 1966); Nurul Islam, "Exchange Control, Liberalization, and Economic Growth in Pakistan," mimeo (1971).

could be imported with bonus vouchers, and toward the end of the 1960's this was true for most imports, but this meant paying an additional 160%-180% premium.

High tariffs in the absence of licensing would have meant a high ceiling to which domestic producers could raise their prices. Import licensing meant that imports would not serve as a check on domestic prices even if domestic producers set prices above the CIF plus tariff levels. The effective ceiling would be reached only when prices reached the CIF plus bonus voucher plus tariff

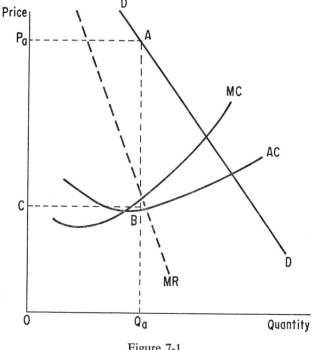

Figure 7-1

levels. There was, then, a substantial barrier to free entry at the marketing end, and domestic producers did
have considerably more room to exercise their market
power than would have been true if imports had been
freely importable.

These conclusions can be demonstrated with the aid
of some simple geometry. Figure 7-1 depicts the standard
textbook monopoly equilibrium.[2] The monopolist faces
a demand curve DD and perceives a marginal revenue
curve MR. He operates with marginal costs MC and

[2] This and all the following results would, of course, hold true
for an oligopoly jointly acting as a monopolist.

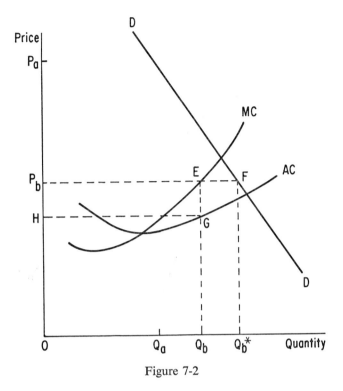

Figure 7-2

average costs AC. He maximizes his profits by expanding his production to quantity Q_a, where marginal costs equal marginal revenues. He charges a price P_a, and he makes monopoly profits equal to the area $P_a ABC$.

In Figure 7-2, foreign competing goods are freely importable at a CIF plus tariff price of P_b. The monopolist cannot raise his price above P_b and thus is prevented from exploiting his monopoly power. The effective demand curve that he faces is $P_b FD$. Price P_b is the price that rules in the market, quantity Q_b is produced domestically, and quantity $Q_b Q_b^*$ is imported. The monopolist's profits have been limited to $P_b EGH$. With a higher tariff, price

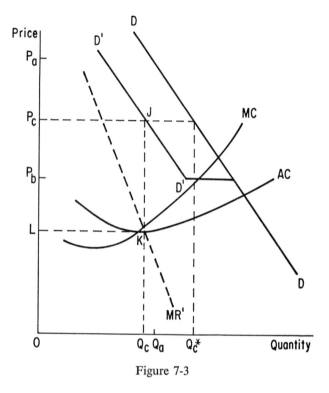

Figure 7-3

P_b would be higher, more would be produced domestically,[3] less would be imported, and the monopolist's profits would increase.

In Figure 7-3, import licenses for only $Q_cQ_c{}^*$ in foreign goods are available at an importer's price (CIF plus tariff) of P_b. The demand schedule $D'D$ now facing the monopolist is parallel to the original but is shifted to the left by the amount $Q_cQ_c{}^*$, since at all prices above the CIF

[3] If the tariff were raised above the point at which imports were completely choked off, domestic output would decline as the monopolist then restricted his output toward his isolated monopoly point.

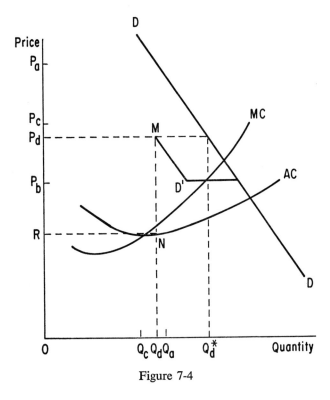

Figure 7-4

plus tariff price of P_b the demand for the monopolist's product is reduced by the amount of the licensed imports. But he is free to charge any price on the new demand schedule, since only $Q_cQ_c{}^*$ can be imported. He will thus produce up to the point where he equates his marginal costs and his new marginal revenue curve MR'. He produces Q_c at a price P_c. His monopoly profits are P_cJKL. The more stringent is the importing licensing, the higher will be the monopolist's output, price, and profits. The holders of the import licenses make a windfall gain of P_c minus P_b on each unit of their imports. Import duties only act to absorb part of their windfall gain but they do not affect the monopolist's output, price, or profits until the duties get high enough to restrict the demand for imports below the licensed level.

In Figure 7-4, import licenses for $Q_d Q_d^*$ in foreign goods at price P_b are available, but additional imports can be imported at the CIF plus bonus vouchers plus tariff price of P_d . This places a price ceiling of P_d on the monopolist and restricts his demand curve to $P_d MD'$. In the figure, he chooses to produce Q_d, with a price P_d that just forestalls the bonus voucher imports. His profits are $P_d MNR$. The height of the tariff, the price of bonus vouchers, and the stringency of licensing would all affect the monopolist's action.

If the domestic producers themselves were the holders of the licenses for the competing imports, then imports would no longer serve as any kind of check on the market power of the domestic producers. The entire market demand would be available to the domestic producers, and the imports would be part of their supply. This was true for a number of firms, since some families controlling the manufacturing firms also controlled importing firms that had the licenses for competing imports. Hyesons Steel Mills, for example, was a dominant producer of galvanized iron pipe, while Hyesons Commercial and Industrial Corp. was the exclusive holder of import licenses for galvanized iron pipe.

Economic Effects: A Simple Model of Profits and a Test

We can now examine some of the economic effects of the oligopoly structure in Pakistani manufacturing. We would expect that profit rates would be higher in those industries in which firms could more easily coordinate their actions and act as a joint monopolist. Monopoly profits would not automatically induce entry at the manufacturing level, since entry required imported capital goods and these required sanctions; the barrier to entry here would be high and subject to the arbitrary actions of the licensing agencies. Thus, the market structure of producing firms would tell us what we needed to know about market power at this level.

Competitive imports could limit profits in an industry, but these were also subject to licensing. Thus, the degree of licensing stringency on competitive imports would be a relevant variable explaining profit rates.

Finally, an important influence on profits would be the terms on which firms could get imported raw materials: the tariffs they have to pay and their ability to get the raw materials freely. The former aspect is related to the notion of effective protection; the total protection given to an industry is related not only to the tariffs on its output but also to the tariff on its inputs.[4] The latter aspect is related to raw materials import licensing. If the licenses for inputs were very stringent, output would be limited to a level below the profit maximizing level. Costs would be high because of the inability to use capacity optimally. With less stringent licensing, profit maximizing levels could be reached. Even an industry with an otherwise competitive structure would find its output limited by the input licenses to monopolistic levels. Finally, with yet looser licensing, competitive firms would be freer to compete with one another, and profits would recede from their monopoly levels.

[4] See William M. Corden, "The Structure of a Tariff System and the Effective Protection Rate," *Journal of Political Economy* (June 1966).

Formally, then, we have a model in which $\pi = f(S, LCM, LIM)$ where π is the profits in an industry, S is a structural variable indicating the ease with which industry members can coordinate their actions, LCM is a variable indicating the relative stringency of licenses for competitive imports, and LIM is a variable indicating the relative stringency of licenses for imported inputs.[5]

A test of this model was made, using cross-section data primarily from 1964 and 1965. The only available profit rates are for firms listed on the Karachi Stock Exchange. These firms were grouped into usable industrial classifications, and the weighted average of their profit rates (net profits before taxes as percentage of net worth) was used.[6] The structural variable was the four-firm concentration ratio.[7] This was the most straightforward and easiest measure to use. Two forms of this variable were tried: the concentration ratio itself, and a 0, 1 dummy variable, with the variable taking a value of 0 for ratios below 33.3% and a value of 1 for ratios above 33.3%. The dummy variable approach was tried because the relationship might be non-linear: there might be some point at which the oligopolists could easily coordinate

[5] This model is similar to the types of models that have been used to explain cross-section profit rates in the United States. For the recent work in this area, see Louis Esposito and Frances Ferguson Esposito, "Foreign Competition and Domestic Industry Profitability," *Review of Economics and Statistics* (November 1971).

[6] Since some firms did and others did not have tax holidays, profits before taxes appeared to be the best measure.

[7] Because of the unavailability of earlier data, the 1968 ratios were used. Though concentration was probably generally lower in 1968 than in 1964, the 1968 figures would be misleading only if the concentration decreases were appreciably greater in some industries over others.

their actions, and greater concentration beyond that point would have no added effect. The relatively low value of 33% as the dividing line was chosen because of the other structural characteristics, like the legality of price-fixing, which made coordination easier.

For the variable measuring the stringency of licensing of competitive imports, I used the figures given by Lewis and Guisinger for the average difference between the domestic price and the CIF import price for the various industries in 1963-1964.[8]

There was no direct measure available for a variable measuring the stringency of licensing of inputs, so instead I used a proxy: the degree of capacity utilization by industry. The degree of capacity utilization was usually limited by raw materials availability.[9] The capacity utili-

[8] I also tried Lewis and Guisinger's figures for the total effective protection by industry, which included the duties on inputs as well as the difference between domestic price and CIF price on the outputs, but unsatisfactory results were achieved. I attribute these results to the high level of aggregation that had to go into the input-output table that underlay Lewis and Guisinger's effective protection calculations. See Stephen R. Lewis, Jr. and Stephen E. Guisinger, "Measuring Protection in a Developing Country: the Case of Pakistan," *Journal of Political Economy* (December 1968). It is interesting to note that this is not the first time that effective protection has been a bad performer. Winston was unable to relate effective protection to capacity utilization in Pakistan. See Gordon C. Winston, "Excess Capacity in Underdeveloped Countries: The Pakistan Case," Research Memorandum No. 25, Center for Development Economics, Williams College, September 1968, p. 71.

[9] Winston's evidence indicates that capacity utilization was strongly related to raw materials availability in Pakistan. See Gordon C. Winston, "Capital Utilization in Economic Development," *Economic Journal* (March 1971), p. 48.

zation data came from a special survey conducted by the Central Statistical Office in 1965.[10] We would expect the relationship between profit rates and this variable to be similar in shape to an inverted parabola: at low rates of capacity utilization profit rates would be low, at intermediate rates they would be higher, and at yet higher rates they would be lower again (because of increased competition in some industries).[11] Hence, both the variable and the square of the variable were included.

We would expect to find a positive relationship between profits and concentration rates and between profits and competitive licensing stringency. An inverted parabola between profits and capacity utilization would lead us to expect a positive relationship between profits and capacity utilization and a negative relationship between profits and the square of capacity utilization.[12]

Because of the limitations on the types of firms listed on the Karachi Exchange and the limited number of industries listed by Lewis and Guisinger, the sample was restricted to 17 industries: cotton textiles, jute textiles, artificial silk textiles, sugar, vegetable ghee, tea blending, paper, leather tanning, motor vehicles, chemicals, petroleum products, cement, other non-metallic minerals,

[10] Government of Pakistan Central Statistical Office, *Report on Survey of Capacity Utilization by Manufacturing Industries, 1965* (Karachi, 1967).

[11] Also, high utilization rates might require the use of older, more costly equipment. A firm might be willing to use this equipment, even if it meant temporarily higher costs and lower profits to keep customers satisfied in the short run.

[12] The formula for an inverted parabola is

$$Y = aX^2 + bX + c,$$

where $a < 0$, $b > 0$, and $c \gtrless 0$.

basic metals, metal products, non-electrical machinery, and electrical machinery.

Before turning to the results of the test, we need to discuss the quality of the data. Virtually all data have quirks and inconsistencies that create difficulties for researchers. The data generated in LDC's tend to contain many more quirks and inconsistencies, and Pakistan is no exception. The average profit rate reported for the 17 industries was 22%. But the profit rates reported by firms on the Karachi Exchange were generally considered to be understatements of the true profits earned. First, accelerated depreciation allowances for tax purposes allowed firms legally to understate true profits. Second, many firms were surrounded by buying, selling, and managing agencies that siphoned off profits from the central firm. These agencies were always private companies wholly owned by the same family that controlled the central firm. Through manipulation of the transfer prices of inputs bought for the firm and of output sold for the firm, these agencies appropriated some of the profits that otherwise would have been shared with the non-family stockholders of the central firm.

For example, the Steel Corporation of Pakistan, Ltd. (SCOP) was a publicly listed company, controlled by the Fancy family but with many other stockholders as well. All of the imported steel inputs for the firm were sold to it by a purchasing agent, Pakistan Industries, Ltd., a company wholly owned by the Fancy family. The output of SCOP was sold through a selling agent, Steel Sales, Ltd., also a Fancy company. The management of SCOP itself was in the hands of a managing agent, Industrial Managements, Ltd., again a Fancy company. The profits listed by SCOP in its publicly available balance sheets were, of course, net of the transfer prices surrounding it. These practices were countenanced by the existing commercial law, the British Companies Act of 1913, which had not been revised since independence. The Pirzada Report of 1962, which recommended a number of substantial revisions in the Companies Act, was never publicly released.

A third contributing factor to the understating of profits was outright lying to evade taxes. This generally took the form of "back-door sales" that were never recorded on the books of the company.

Publicly reported profits, then, were understatements. Were they, as a consequence, random? Or did they bear some systematic relationship to the underlying profitability of the firm? I believe the latter is true, though only a knowledge of the true balance sheet data could completely verify this. There were advantages for the controllers of a firm in revealing healthy profits and having a favorable price for the publicly quoted shares of stock of their firm. It was easier to raise future capital, and it was easier and more lucrative to sell off some of their holdings if they wanted. Further, there were surely limits on how far tax evasion and profits hiding could go, and I suspect these limits were more related to the profits themselves than to any absolute levels. Reported profits, then, were probably related to true profits, though the relationship was a good deal less precise than one finds, for example, in comparable American data.

There are other limitations on the data. Some of the limitations on the use of four-firm concentration ratios have been discussed earlier. Since the industrial classifications used in the test were broad, some personal judgment had to be used in deciding how to characterize an industry with a single concentration ratio. The Lewis and Guisinger price differentials were averages for these same broad categories, and one runs the risk that these averages might be inappropriate for specialized components within the broad categories. Also, to the extent that companies were engaged in exporting and practiced price discrimination between their export and their protected domestic markets, the Lewis and Guisinger figures (based on domestic prices only) probably overstate the average price differential. Finally, capacity utilization figures are always subject to error, since "full capacity" itself is a slippery concept. The CSO capacity survey may have been less than perfect in its attempt to get consistent concepts of full capacity across different industries.[13]

The data, then, are imperfect, and one ought not to expect perfect results from them. On the other hand, one ought not, necessarily, to throw up one's hands and abandon all hope of systematic investigation.

The model presented above was tested through the use of ordinary least squares regressions. The result of the regression were as follows (the numbers in parentheses are t-ratios):

(1) $\Pi = -0.37 + 0.16\,S_1 + 0.08\,DM$
        (0.68)   (1.74)   (2.25)
    $+1.19\,CU - 0.81\,CU^2$
    (0.73)   (0.70) $R^2 = 0.42$

(2) $\Pi = -0.55 + 0.15\,S_2 + 0.07\,DM$
        (1.91)   (2.09)   (2.19)
    $+ 1.80\,CU - 1.27\,CU^2$
    (1.08)   (1.07) $R^2 = 0.47$

[13] See Warren P. Hogan, "Capacity Creation and Utilization in Pakistan Manufacturing Industry," *Australian Economic Papers* (June 1968).

where Π is the pre-tax net profit on net worth by industry (average value: 22%), S_1 is the four-firm concentration ratio (average: 63%), S_2 is a 0,1 dummy variable dividing the concentration ratio at 33.3%, DM is the percentage by which domestic prices exceeded CIF import prices (average: 114%), and CU is capacity utilization (average: 68%).

The signs of the coefficients in both equations are those which the model predicts. The magnitude of the coefficients on S_1 and S_2 are reasonable, though perhaps a trifle high. The coefficient on DM is surely too low, though it does point in the right direction. As noted above, price discrimination in export markets may account for part of this low bias. The coefficients on CU and CU^2 are most reasonable. They indicate that maximum profit rates were reached at a capacity utilization rate of 70%-75%.[14] The R^2 term indicates that over 40% of the variability in profit rates can be explained by the model. Since the profit rates have a great deal of "noise" in them to begin with, these results are encouraging.

The results, then, indicate that there seems to be a positive relationship between profit rates, industrial concentration, and import licensing stringency. The sample is small, the data are spotty, and the results are not wholly satisfactory, but the basic tendencies seem to be present.

Profit Rates and Sanctioned Entry

High profit rates would normally induce entry by new firms, but entry was controlled by the sanctioning agen-

[14] The maximum for an inverted parabola is given by the formula $-\dfrac{b}{2a}$. This is, then, for equation (1): $\dfrac{-1.19}{(2)(-0.81)} = 0.73$.

cies. Were the sanctioning agencies sensitive to profit rates and did they sanction new capacity and new competition in areas where profit rates were high?

A partial test of this proposition is possible. In 1966 the central government released a Comprehensive Industrial Investment Schedule, showing the government's sanctioning intentions concerning the expansion of industrial capacity for the Third Five-Year Plan (1965-1970).[15] The percentage increase of intended capacity over existing capacity was regressed against profit rates for 17 industries,[16] with the following results:

$$(3) \quad EX = 0.48 + 0.15 \, \Pi$$
$$\qquad\quad (2.52) \quad (0.17) \qquad\qquad R^2 = 0.00$$

where EX is the intended percentage expansion of an industry (average: 51%) and Π is the pre-tax net profit on net worth of the industry (average: 19%). The regression shows virtually no relationship between intended expansion and profit rates. To further test the possible intentions of the central government, the extent of capacity utilization by industry and the percentage of total industry supply provided by imports were added to the regression, with the following results:

$$(4) \quad EX = 0.81 + 0.22 \, \Pi - 0.36 \, CU - 0.35 \, MP$$
$$\qquad\quad (2.03) \quad (0.22) \quad\; (0.83) \qquad (1.00)$$
$$\qquad\qquad\qquad\qquad\qquad\qquad\qquad R^2 = 0.07$$

where CU is the capacity utilization rate (average: 70%) and MP is the percentage of imports in industry supply

[15] Government of Pakistan, Department of Investment, Promotion, and Supplies, *Comprehensive Industrial Investment Schedule for Third Five-Year Plan (1965-70)* (Karachi, 1966).

[16] Two industries—motor vehicles and petroleum—were dropped from the previous sample of 17 because of unavailable data, but cigarettes and woolen textiles were added.

(average: 28%). One would expect the coefficients on these last two variables to be positive, since high rates of capacity utilization would seem to call for more capacity, and high import percentages might appear to offer a ripe field for import substitution. But the coefficients are in fact negative and insignificant, and the coefficient on profit rates does not become appreciably more significant. There may have been a method to the central government's expansion intentions, but observed profit rates, capacity utilization, or import percentages do not seem to have been among the criteria used.

Economic Effects—Innovation

Virtually nothing is known about research and development in Pakistan. We do not know how much is undertaken, who does it, and what are its effects. The only figures available are for patent applications in Pakistan. These figures are presented in Table 7-3. The number of patent applications from Pakistani inventors has been around only 100 a year; the remainder has been from foreign inventors and corporations filing to protect their foreign patents. Some of the Pakistani applications have come from universities and research institutions, so the patent applications by private Pakistani inventors has been yet smaller than the number in the table. If the industrial concentration in Pakistan has had any positive effects on research and development and technological change, it has yet to be reflected in the patent statistics.

Economic Effects of Overall Concentration

The large industrial families and groups dominated the industrial structure of Pakistan. They received the lion's share of the licenses for industrial investment. What

TABLE 7-3
Patent Applications in Pakistan

	Patent Applications by Pakistanis	Patent Applications by Foreigners
1957	43	981
1958	27	1,023
1959	48	1,103
1960	61	1,062
1961	54	1,063
1962	80	1,115
1963	94	1,134
1964	110	1,164
1965	103	1,198
1966	158	1,280
1967	111	1,166
1968	81	1,199
1969	88	1,130

SOURCE: M. A. Toor, "Patents as Instruments of the Flow of Technology from Developed to Developing Countries," *Trade and Industry* (July-August 1970).

effects did this have on the size and operation of their companies?

To explore this question, I took a sample of firms from those listed on the Karachi Stock Exchange. Of the 191 non-financial firms listed in 1968, there were 98 manufacturing firms controlled by private Pakistani entrepreneurs and listed for five years or more. To avoid the erratic effects of the starting-up problems of young firms, I focused on these "seasoned" companies. Of these companies, 65 were controlled by the leading industrial families and the remaining 33 were controlled by Pakistani entrepreneurs who were not among the leading families. Table 7-4 summarizes some of the important characteristics of the companies controlled by the two groups.

TABLE 7-4

Average Characteristics of a Sample of 98 Manufacturing
Companies Listed on the Karachi Stock Exchange

	Companies Controlled by the 43 Largest Families and Groups	Other Private Domestically Controlled Companies
Number	65	33
Age of company, as of 1968	13.1 years	11.4 years
Number of years on Karachi Stock Exchange	8.9 years	6.7 years
Total assets per firm, 1968	Rs.58.9 million	Rs.16.2 million
Sales per firm, 1968	Rs.53.4 million	Rs.18.9 million
Profit rates,[a] 1964-1968, unweighted	15.4%	11.6%
Profit rates,[a] 1964-1968, weighted[b]	16.6%	12.9%
Growth of assets, 1964-1968, unweighted	72.6%	64.1%
Growth of assets, 1964-1968, weighted[c]	41.5%	41.9%
Growth of sales, 1964-1968, weighted[d]	80.6%	79.8%

[a] Net profits before taxes as a percentage of net worth.
[b] Weighted by current year net worth.
[c] Weighted by 1964 assets.
[d] Weighted by 1964 sales.

SOURCE: State Bank of Pakistan, *Balance Sheet Analysis of Joint Stock Companies Listed on the Karachi Stock Exchange 1964-69* (Karachi, 1971).

The firms controlled by the leading industrial families tended to be slightly older than the non-family firms. They were three times as large in average size of assets and of sales. They were more profitable, and they generally grew faster than did non-family firms.

I used regression analysis to try to analyze these differences and to study systematic relationships. First, what determined the size of these 98 firms? The most powerful

explanatory variable, not too surprisingly, was the original equity capital that was used to establish the firm, as is
seen in equation (5):

$$(5) \quad A8 = 9.68 + 4.10 \, OE$$
$$(2.64)(15.26) \qquad R^2 = 0.71$$

where $A8$ is the total assets of a firm in 1968 (average:
Rs.44.5 million) and OE is the original equity of the firm
at the time it was listed on the exchange (average: Rs.8.5
million). Efforts to explain the size of firms by industrial
classifications, attempted by adding to the above equation
dummy variables (0,1) representing a firm's membership,
in an industry proved unsuccessful; the addition of the
age of the firm was equally unproductive. Even the addition of a dummy variable representing control by the
leading industrial family proved only mildly significant,
as is indicated by equation (6):

$$(6) \quad A8 = 3.34 + 3.91 \, OE + 11.85 \, F$$
$$(0.68)(13.83) \qquad (1.85)$$
$$R^2 = 0.72$$

where F is a 0,1 dummy variable indicating whether or
not a firm is controlled by a leading industrial family. A
similar, though weaker, pattern was found for the size of
sales for a firm in 1968.

The original equity capital, in turn, was determined by
the resources an entrepreneur could muster and the investment license he could expect to receive. Here, family
control of firms does seem to have been important, as is
seen in equation (7):

$$(7) \quad OE = 3.26 + 7.89 \, F$$
$$(1.85) \ (3.65) \qquad R^2 = 0.12$$

Average profit rates for firms between 1964 and 1968
do not seem to have been related to the size of the firm,

industry membership, or family control. Differences in profit rates among firms seem to have been largely a random phenomenon. Given the vagaries of the licensing system (and of individual company accounting practices), this is not too surprising.[17]

The growth of assets by firm between 1964 and 1968 was strongly related to the profits of the firm. Looking first at the growth of total assets by firm and comparing it to net profits, we find the following relationship:

$$(8) \quad GA = -0.31 + 3.55\,NP(A)$$
$$\quad\quad\quad (1.31)\ (5.33) \quad\quad\quad\quad R^2 = 0.23$$

where GA is the growth of total assets (average: 70% and $NP(A)$ is the after-tax net profits earned by the firm between 1965 and 1968 divided by the total assets of the firm in 1964 (average: 0.23).[18] This indicates that every marginal rupee in after-tax profits generated Rs.-3.55 in additional assets—from reinvestment, new flotation of equity capital, and additional loans and credits. The performance by the family and non-family controlled firms is shown by the following two equations:

$$(8a)\ \text{(family firms)} \quad GA = -0.52 + 4.41\,NP(A)$$
$$\quad\quad\quad\quad\quad\quad (1.50)\ (4.38)$$
$$\quad\quad\quad\quad\quad\quad\quad\quad\quad\quad R^2 = 0.23$$

$$(8b)\ \text{(non-family firms)} \quad GA = -0.03 + 2.36\,NP(A)$$
$$\quad\quad\quad\quad\quad\quad\quad (0.12)\ (4.12)$$
$$\quad\quad\quad\quad\quad\quad\quad\quad\quad\quad R^2 = 0.35$$

[17] This does not run contrary to the earlier results explaining industry profit rates for 1964-1965. These profit rates by firm are over a five-year time period, during which many more influences came to bear on the firms.

[18] Both the absolute growth of assets and the profits of the firm have been standardized across firms by dividing each by the total assets of the firm in 1966. Only profits for the years 1965 through 1968 were used, since profits from the 1964 ac-

The firms controlled by the industrial families seem to have been somewhat better able to parlay their profits into greater assets, but a Chow F-test indicates that the difference in the coefficients is not significant at a 95% confidence level.[19] Again, efforts to include dummy variables representing the industrial classification of a firm yielded no significant results.

By next looking at the relationship between the growth of net worth and the profits of these firms, we can get some idea of the private saving rates connected with these firms, since increases in net worth could come only from reinvested profits or flotations of new equity requiring savings by the new investors:

$$(9) \quad GNW = -0.05 + 0.88 \, NP(NW)$$
$$ (0.81) \, (12.76) \qquad R^2 = 0.61$$

where GNW is the growth of new worth (average: 47%) and $NP(NW)$ is the profits earned by the firm between 1965 and 1968, divided by the net worth of the firm in 1964. This equation indicates that for every extra rupee of net profit, Rs.0.88 in extra equity was generated from reinvestment and new flotation. Looking at the performance of the family and non-family firms, we find:

$$(9a) \quad \text{(family)} \qquad GNW = -0.10 + 0.93 \, NP(NW)$$
$$\phantom{(9a) \quad \text{(family)} \qquad GNW = } (1.28) \, (9.94)$$
$$\phantom{(9a) \quad \text{(family)} \qquad GNW = (1.28) \, (9.94) } R^2 = 0.60$$

$$(9b) \quad \text{(non-family)} \quad GNW = -0.01 + 0.83 \, NP(NW)$$
$$\phantom{(9b) \quad \text{(non-family)} \quad GNW = } (0.16) \, (9.89)$$
$$\phantom{(9b) \quad \text{(non-family)} \quad GNW = (0.16) \, (9.89) } R^2 = 0.63$$

counting year would have already had their effect on the assets listed for 1964.

[19] See Gregory C. Chow, "Tests of Equality Between Sets of Coefficients in Two Linear Regressions," *Econometrica* (July 1960).

Again, the Chow test indicates that the difference in the performance of family and non-family firms was not significantly different.

These findings indicate that the large industrial families did not perform significantly better than did the other private entrepreneurs in the economy. The evidence here does not offer any justification for the special treatment that these families received. These equations do indicate, however, generally high rates of reinvestment-cum-new-flotation. The strategy of the government of Pakistan at the time of creating and encouraging high profits in the hope that they would be saved and reinvested appears to have been successful. Unfortunately, since true profits were surely much higher than reported profits, we do not know what the true reinvestment rates were. Somewhat counterbalancing this, additional profits were being invested in newly formed enterprises that were excluded from this sample.

But the *social benefit* of the entire strategy was highly doubtful. The very high rates of effective protection that generated those profits were probably indicative of unfavorable social benefit-cost ratios when the opportunity costs to Pakistan (i.e., world prices) were taken into consideration. Little, Scitovsky, and Scott found that the contribution of large scale manufacturing to Pakistani growth was "negligible."[20] Even within the context of the strategy, the government's regional goals for private investment were not met. The five-year plans had aimed for a 50-50 division of private investment between East and West Pakistan. But in the 1960's the regional division of new investment was consistently 25-75.[21] As we

[20] Ian Little, Tibor Scitovsky, and Maurice Scott, *Industry and Trade in Some Developing Countries* (London, 1970), pp. 74-75.
[21] Government of Pakistan, Planning Commission, *Evaluation*

saw in Chapter 4, the leading industrial families themselves had only a quarter of their assets in East Pakistan.

In the end, as was discussed earlier in Chapter 2, the primary beneficiaries of economic growth in Pakistan's labor surplus economy were the industrialists themselves. Reinvestment was far from a philanthropic activity.

Non-Economic Effects—Influence and Power

The leading industrial families and groups were not passive recipients of the benefits of government policies. A number of them had an active hand in formulating and even administering these policies. A number of the family members were ministers in the central government and ambassadors abroad at various times. They were frequently appointed by the government as members of special committees to study problems and recommend policies concerning industrial matters. By itself, this would not be considered exceptional behavior by a government. Businessmen are frequently appointed to committees and commissions by the American and other Western governments. But there were few other interested groups or sources of power to offset the influence of the businessmen. Labor and consumer groups did not exist, and independent academic expertise in economics was in very short supply. Agricultural interests posed the only threat to business interests. The large rural landlords were a powerful force within the Pakistani polity, and many of the high ranking officials in the civil service and the army had their roots, or at least their sympathies, in agriculture. But the manufacturing interests, aided by the ideological power of modernization and development

---

of the Third Five-Year Plan (1965-70) (Rawalpindi, 1971), pp. 21-22.

that the growth of industry implied, were generally able to control the field on crucial questions like the duties and taxes that would affect the internal terms of trade for agricultural and manufactured products.[22] Manufactured goods received high levels of protection, explicitly through high tariffs, quotas, import bans, and export subsidies, while agricultural goods were subject to explicit export taxes and implicit taxation through the existence of the overvalued exchange rate. In return, though, the large landlords were able to obtain a blanket exemption of agricultural incomes from income tax.

The political power of the large industrial families could also be seen in the squashing or suppressing of government reports and actions that would have limited their economic power. There were three important reports in the early 1960's that were never released: the Pirzada Report in 1962, which recommended revising the Companies Act, giving minority stockholders greater power and limiting the inside dealing and chicanery that the controllers of a company could engage in; the Cartel Study Group Report of 1963, which discussed the extent of industrial concentration and economic power in the economy; and the report by Louis Loss in 1964, which recommended much tighter regulation of the stock exchanges and securities markets. There was widespread knowledge of the existence of these reports and their general nature, but the absence of the reports themselves severely limited the intelligent discussion of these issues. Further, the one attempt by the Minister of Finance in

[22] For a further discussion of the terms of trade between agriculture and manufacturing, see Stephen R. Lewis, Jr., "The Effects of Trade Policy on Domestic Relative Prices: Pakistan, 1951-1965," *American Economic Review* (March 1968).

1963 to encourage wider ownership of existing companies, through a tax on tightly held companies, was beaten
down by the Karachi business community.

An indication of the influence of the leading families
on the administration of policy, as it affected the families
themselves, is their representation on important government bodies. The families' representation on the board
of directors of the Pakistan Industrial Credit and Investment Corporation, and their success in obtaining investment sanctions from that organization, has already been
detailed in Chapter 6. The leading industrial families
were also represented on the boards of directors of the
State Bank of Pakistan (the central bank), the Pakistan
Insurance Corporation, the National Bank of Pakistan,
and other government-controlled corporations. Their
representation is listed in Table 7-5.

As an additional example of the interplay of economic
power and political influence, we can look at the actions
of the large government-managed mutual fund (unit
trust), the National Investment Trust (NIT). Of the 13
men on the NIT board of directors, 7 represented the
government or the quasi-public development banks and
institutions. The remaining 6 represented private banks
and industrial activities. All of these 6 were representatives from the leading industrial families. The chairman
was Mr. Ahmed Dawood.

NIT had a portfolio worth Rs.142.7 million in 1968,
of which Rs.131.6 million was invested in the shares and
securities of non-financial corporations. Of this last figure,
71.1% was invested in securities issued by firms controlled by the important industrial families. As was seen
in Table 4-5, the firms controlled by the leading industrial families constituted only 47.9% of all the assets of

TABLE 7-5

Membership on the Boards of Directors of Government-Controlled
Companies by the Leading Industrial Families, 1968

	Total Number of Directors	Number of Directors from Leading Families
Pakistan Industrial Credit and Investment Corp.	21	7
Pakistan Insurance Corp.	9	6
State Bank of Pakistan	13	2
National Bank of Pakistan	12	3 (president)
Bank of Bahawalpur	10	3
Zeal Pak Cement (WPIDC)	9	4
Harnai Woolen Mills (WPIDC)	4	0
National Shipping Corp.	9	1
Pakistan International Airlines	7	2
Pakistan House International	14	7 (chairman)
Pakistan Services	18	10
Platinum Jubilee Jute Mills (EPIDC)	5	0
National Investment Trust	13	6

SOURCES: Iqbal Haidari and Abdul Hafeez Khan, *Stock Exchange Guide of Pakistan*, rev. edn. (Karachi, 1968); Karachi Stock Exchange, *Year Book* (Karachi, 1968).

non-financial companies listed on the Karachi and Dacca Exchanges. NIT's investments, then, were heavily skewed in favor of the companies of the leading families.

Presumably, a primary objective of NIT was to maximize the value of its portfolio. Perhaps the family-controlled companies were indeed the best companies in which NIT should have invested. If so, this underlines the dilemma that the industrial groups who received a head start were then the "natural" recipients of further support and encouragement. But NIT did not have a passive role on the stock exchanges. Rather, as the major buyer and holder of shares on the exchanges, NIT was a major force in determining the prices of shares and hence had an influence on the value of its own portfolio. Different portfolio strategies might have been pursued with equal success.

In sum, the leading industrial families were actively involved and influential in the political and administrative processes that directly affected their industrial interests. From their economic power base, they were able to attain positions and influence that served to maintain and expand that base.

Income Distribution, Taxation, and Development Effort

Thus far in this study we have focused exclusively on the assets controlled by the leading industrial families. These assets were yielding a substantial income for the families, with important distributional implications and larger political implications. This section will attempt to estimate these incomes and discuss their implications.

The estimates of Chapter 4 indicated that the 43 largest industrial families and groups controlled Rs.6,314.6 million in manufacturing assets in 1967-1968. They controlled an additional Rs.142.1 million in assets in transportation, utilities, and mining assets, for a total of Rs.6,456.7 million in industrial assets. It is impossible to determine exactly what fraction of the assets controlled by the families and groups represented net ownership. But the net worth of the listed corporations was approximately half of total assets, and a figure of 60% for the families' ownership percentage of the listed firms and 100% of wholly owned firms appears reasonable.[23] This

---

[23] The resulting net worth figures are in reasonable agreement with some independent estimates of some of the families' net worth made by some individuals close to the Karachi business scene. In 1963, 75% of the shares of publicly listed companies

yields a figure for the families' industrial net worth of Rs.2,175 million. To this, we should add 60% of the net worth of publicly listed banks and insurance companies controlled by the families, and 100% of the wholly owned financial institutions. The families' net worth in these banks and insurance companies in 1968 was approximately Rs.195 million. The sum of their industrial and financial net worth came to Rs.2,370 million. This still excluded the families' interests in trading companies and managing agencies and their portfolio wealth, but estimates of these figures would be truly wild guesses.

What kind of return did the families earn on these assets? A figure of 20% after taxes on net worth would be considered a very conservative figure by most observers, particularly considering the legal tax loopholes like accelerated depreciation and the widespread illegal tax evasion that occurred.[24] Since we have not been able to include the income from the buying, selling, and managing agencies that these families employed to surround their publicly listed firms and siphon off profits, this is indeed a conservative figure.

This 20% rate would have yielded an annual income to the families of Rs.474 million. In 1967-1968 Pakistan's net national product at factor cost was estimated

---

were in the hands of the controllers of these firms, with another 20% in the hands of institutions, and only 5% in the hands of the general public. See *Finance and Industry* (March 1964), p. 19. By 1968, tax pressures and institutional expansion had probably reduced the average controlling interest to 60%.

[24] The 65 "seasoned" manufacturing firms controlled by these families showed a weighted rate of return on net worth of 19.1% "before provision for taxes." But frequently the provision for taxes was mythical, and the factors cited in the text surely would have raised the true rate of return.

to be Rs.57,406 million. Thus, these 43 industrial families and groups, representing roughly one two-thousandths of 1% of the population,[25] had four-fifths of 1% of net national product.

Bergan, in a careful study of Pakistani income and expenditure data, concluded that in 1963-1964 the top fifth of all income recipients received 45% of all income, the top 10% received 30%, and the top 5% received 20%.[26] For urban income receivers only, the distribution was even more skewed, with the top 20% receiving 52%, the top 10% receiving 37%, and the top 5% receiving 26% of all income. Another way of expressing this last figure is that the top 5% received an average income that was five times the average urban income in Pakistan. We now see that the upper tail of the income distribution beyond the 5% point was, not surprisingly, yet more skewed. The top one two-thousandths of 1% received incomes 1,600 times the average income in Pakistan.

Since the average income in Pakistan itself was being pulled up by the very high incomes, a comparison to the median income might be somewhat more meaningful. The median income for income receivers was approximately 70% of the average income. Thus the top one two-thousandth of 1% of the population had incomes 2,300 times the median income in Pakistan.

I believe that this top-heavy income distribution had important consequences for the political complexion of Pakistan and particularly for its taxation policies. The urban middle class in Pakistan constantly had before it

[25] Counting wives, children, and close relations, these groups at most represented 500-600 people.

[26] Asbjorn Bergan, "Personal Income Distribution and Personal Savings in Pakistan, 1963/64," *Pakistan Development Review* (Summer 1967).

the example of the very wealthy industrialists who quite clearly had succeeded. The sumptuous houses and fancy automobiles of the rich were in public view; the wheelings and dealings of their companies were frequently in the newspapers. With this example before them, the middle class strongly resisted all taxation, especially all direct taxation of income. Undoubtedly, no one likes to be taxed, and urban middle classes around the world have resisted taxation. But in a general atmosphere of much greater income equality within Pakistan, I believe that the resistance to taxation would have been considerably less.

As it was, the personal income tax in Pakistan was studded with exemptions and reductions and its incidence started at a comparatively high income. Only incomes above Rs.6,000 were liable to taxation. For a family of six, Rs.6,000 represented an income that was twice the national average. An additional Rs.3,000-Rs.5,000 of dividend income was exempted, as was Rs.5,000 from government securities and Rs.6,000 from rents from newly constructed residences. Further exemptions were granted for income that was devoted to investments in new companies, and capital gains held from six months to five years were taxed at one-third the normal rate and at one-sixth the normal rate after five years. A taxpayer could even deduct Rs.360 a year for the maintenance of a motorcycle or scooter and Rs.900-Rs.1,500 for the maintenance of an automobile. The marginal tax rate in 1968-1969 on taxable income began at 2% and reached 17.5% at Rs.6,500, reached 47.5% at Rs.30,000, and reached the ceiling of 70% at Rs.100,000.[27] Finally, all income from agricultural sources was exempt.

[27] These rates were below the rates in effect in 1959-1960, though they were above the rates of the middle 1950's.

Given this structure, it is not surprising that in 1964-1965, the most recent year for which figures are available, only 113,826 individuals paid personal income taxes.[28] This represented less than 1% of the households in the country. The total income that was subject to taxation was Rs.899.5 million, only 2% of GNP in 1964-1965; even if we exclude agricultural income that was totally exempt, taxable incomes were only 4% of non-agricultural GNP.

The corporation tax was similarly studded with exemptions and areas of favorable treatment, especially for depreciation allowances, and it also had a number of important rate reductions. The nominal rate was 60% (income tax and super tax combined), but banks and insurance companies received a rebate of 5%, publicly listed companies received a rebate of 10%, and income distributed as dividends received an additional rebate of 15%. Companies involved in processing food received an extra 10% rebate, and income earned abroad gained a 15% rebate. Companies investing in most areas outside Karachi received a 4-6 year tax holiday from the time of the start of operations. Rab estimated that nearly one-third of corporate income was exempt because of tax holidays.[29] The corporate tax figures indicate that the tax paid on taxable income (net of tax holidays and of special depreciation allowances) was at an average rate of 47.9%. If we include the tax holidays and allowances, corporate taxes paid were surely less than 30% of profits.

Surrounding the personal and corporate tax systems

[28] Government of Pakistan, Ministry of Finance, Central Board of Revenue, *All-Pakistan Income-Tax Reports and Returns* (Karachi, 1971).

[29] Abdur Rab, "Income Taxation in Pakistan," unpublished Ph.D. thesis, Harvard University, 1967.

was widespread and generally acknowledged tax evasion. There is no way to estimate the total magnitudes involved. However, the tax figures for 1964-1965 indicate legally recognized accumulated tax arrears that were twice as large as direct tax payments that year. Only 75% of the direct taxes assessed that year were actually paid. If these were the figures that were legally acknowledged, the true evasion was surely much higher. This, in addition to the legal structure of the tax system, also helps to account for the small numbers of individuals paying taxes and the apparently small base on which the taxes were levied.

We can use the estimated income figures for the 43 largest industrial families and groups to illustrate further the erosion of the tax base created by legal exemptions and illegal evasion. The estimated income after corporate taxes on the industrial assets of these groups alone was Rs.474 million in 1968. If income tax had been paid at the top rate of 70%,[30] Rs.331.8 million in taxes would have been due. This is an overestimate, since some of the income represented profits retained in companies and not subject to personal income tax, though it was subject to the corporate tax. But the total of personal income taxes and corporate taxes collected from *everyone* in Pakistan came to only Rs.268.1 million in 1967-1968 and only Rs.223.8 million in 1968-1969, and these figures were supposed to include the taxes on the corporate profits of the companies controlled by the largest families, as well as taxes on their personal incomes. There was clearly a great deal of legal and illegal evasion.

[30] This was the marginal rate on incomes over Rs.100,000. If 200 individuals from the 43 families filed tax returns, only Rs.20 million of the Rs.474 million would have been subject to lower tax rates, so the 70% figure is a good approximation.

The consequences of this tax structure and behavior were straightforward. Government revenues, from taxes and other sources, remained below 7% of GNP during the entire 1950's and early 1960's. Only in the late 1960's, with the spur of defense spending generated by the 1965 war with India, did the figure rise significantly, reaching 8.8% in the 1969-1970 fiscal year. Government revenues from direct taxes—income taxes and corporation taxes—reached an absolute and relative peak in 1958-1959 of Rs.398.1 million, for 20.3% of government revenues in that year. They declined steadily in the following years until, in 1968-1969, direct taxes constituted only 3.9% of government revenues. The bulk of government revenues at all times came from indirect taxes: customs duties, sales taxes, and excise taxes.

By international standards, Pakistan had one of the poorer records among LDC's in generating tax revenues and an equally poor one in levying direct taxes. Chelliah found that Pakistan ranked forty-sixth out of 50 LDC's in its ratio of taxes to GNP in the late 1960's, and it ranked forty-third in an index of tax effort (which took into account the level and sectoral composition of the GNP of a country).[31] It ranked fortieth in its ratio of direct taxes to GNP, and it ranked fortieth also in its ratio of direct taxes to total taxes collected.

In sum, Pakistan's performance in generating tax revenues was far from outstanding, and the taxes that it did manage to collect were primarily regressive indirect taxes rather than direct taxes. Further, over 50% of the budget was devoted to defense expenditures. With a poor tax effort, with agricultural incomes (representing half of Pakistan's GNP) exempt, and with defense absorbing

[31] Raja J. Chelliah, "Trends in Taxation in Developing Countries," *IMF Staff Papers* (July 1971).

over half of what was collected, government expenditure on development and health-education-welfare items was severely restricted. And when spending did occur on items like housing, water systems, medical facilities, and schools, the rich and the urban middle class received the lion's share of the benefits.

This could have been otherwise. Though Pakistan was definitely shortchanged in its receipt of administrative facilities and personnel at the time of Partition, the civil administrative bureaucracy that it did inherit from the British was better than most among LDC's. It could have enforced a more stringent tax system that relied more on direct taxes. But the political will of the country was lacking.

Chapter 8

Policies and Problems

THE intertangled knot of monopoly power, economic power, political power, and income distribution creates extremely difficult problems for any country, and they seem to be especially difficult for LDC's. This study has documented the extent, origins, and effects of industrial concentration and economic power in one LDC, Pakistan. I strongly suspect that similar studies for other LDC's would reveal the same broad picture, even though the individual details might be quite different.

Are there useful policy prescriptions that can be offered to deal with these problems? I believe that there are. The first section of this chapter sets out two models of "pure" economic systems that would solve these problems. The following section offers some specific, realistic policies that could be employed. The remainder of the chapter discusses the policies that Pakistan has in fact employed.

Two Extreme Models

I can conceive of two "pure" economic systems that would come to terms with the problems discussed in this book. These are extreme models, on opposite ends of the economic spectrum, and they are not meant to represent the true operation of any actual economic system. But they do allow us to see the basic mechanisms at work.

At the one extreme, one could have a perfectly competitive capitalist system. For an LDC, the heart of this system would have to be a rigidly enforced progressive income tax and a reasonably open foreign trade sector, with modest tariff levels dealing with the domestic market imperfections that might rule out completely free trade. Import licensing would be foresworn in the interests of keeping the barriers to entry low at both the producing and marketing stages. Something close to a flexible exchange rate would be necessary to maintain equilibrium in the balance of payments. One would rely on competition from domestic and foreign producers to keep profits at reasonable levels. A workable antitrust and anti-restrictive practices law might provide some supplementary benefit, but I am doubtful as to the applicability of the American antitrust experience to other legal systems and traditions. One would rely on the progressive income tax to keep the income distribution and economic power within bounds. The role of government in this scheme, beyond enforcing the progressive tax system and pursuing sensible overall monetary and fiscal policies, would be restricted to the provision of social overhead capital— roads, ports, schools, medical facilities—where the externalities appear to be great or the capital requirements are extremely large. The government would also ensure that the barriers to entry in all industries remained low to all comers.

The logic of the Lewis labor surplus model indicates that for many LDC's one could not rely on government expenditure to improve directly the incomes of the bulk of the agricultural and urban working population. Any effort to aid directly the incomes of, say, the urban working population through minimum wages or housing would either be eliminated by the competitive pressure of general unemployment or would serve as an impediment to faster absorption of unemployed labor or both. Rather, one would rely on the expansion of both the agricultural and non-agricultural sectors, combined with the absence of incentives for capital intensive production and perhaps even mild incentives for labor intensive production, to absorb the surplus labor and lead slowly to increases in income per capita based on accumulations of capital per capita, efficient use of existing resources, and on technological progress. The only way that the government could affect and benefit the bulk of the agricultural and urban working population would be by spending money on items that would not normally enter into the expenditure budgets of these groups and hence would not normally be eliminated by the competitive pressure of unemployment. Schooling, health facilities (e.g., adequate water treatment and sewage facilities), and medical care (including an effective family planning program) would appear to be the prime candidates for this type of expenditure.[1]

This kind of purely competitive system would be far from easy to maintain. Progressive income taxes always run the risk of choking off or discouraging productive effort. It is not easy to run an efficient, effective income tax system. This is an information- and skill-intensive endeavor, and LDC's are short of both. The commitment to the absence of import and investment licensing and to keeping the barriers to entry low would have to be somehow etched deeply into the foundations of the polity

[1] Housing would probably not be a good candidate, since it is an important budget item. The provision of subsidized housing by the government would either lead to black-market rents if there was a shortage of these units or to lower money wages if a large number of units were actually built.

of the country, so that temporary accumulations of economic power and political power could not be used to change "the rules of the game" so as to preserve that power.[2] One would probably want to allow some foreign investment into the country to supplement some of the skills and capital available domestically. The absence of excessive protection and the existence of an effective tax system, though, would serve to keep foreign investment flows moderate and prevent most of the abuses and unhappiness that foreign investment has generated in many LDC's.

The provision of capital and the structure of the banking system presents another serious problem in this kind of system. Capital, as a scarce resource and as one of the important components of the ability of any entrepreneur to enter an industry, has a special place in any economy. Yet, with the future uncertain and hence the success or failure of any undertaking subject to uncertainty, some kind of judgment is necessary as to who shall qualify for loans. Who shall have the power to exercise that judgment? If the banking system itself were perfectly competitive, so that potential entrepreneurs had many alternative sources of funds and the judgment power was widely dispersed, one could be less concerned about this problem. But one is more likely to be faced with an oligopolistic banking structure.[3] Here, one would have to try to keep the banking system as competitive as possible and relatively free from direct interlocks with the other sectors of the economy and act directly to correct any gross malfeasances.

---

[2] Along with the commitment to open entry, there would have to be the willingness to see companies fail if they made mistakes.

[3] It is an interesting question whether "natural" economies

At the other extreme, one could construct an economic system that was wholly centrally planned. Virtually all enterprises would be government-owned. All major and most minor economic decisions would be made by the government, at various levels. The day-to-day running of the economy would be under government direction, as would capital accumulation, investment, and development. Personal property would be largely limited to personal belongings. Private monopolies could not arise. Significant accretions of private economic power would be unlikely to occur, and the distribution of income would be under the direct control of the government through its ability to set wages and prices.

This kind of system would be highly dependent on good means of gathering, organizing, and transmitting large amounts of economic information so that informed decisions could be made. But, again, these are skills and facilities in short supply in most LDC's. Decision-making could be decentralized within this kind of system, so as to economize on information transmission needs, but this runs the risk of lower levels of government making conflicting decisions and one loses the advantage of centralized coordination. In principle, one could allow consumer sovereignty, tempered by appropriate taxes and subsidies, to determine the demand for goods and services and allow the government factory manager or farm manager to make short-run allocation decisions in response, while long-run investment decisions and allocations remained centralized.

The existence of thousands, or hundreds of thousands, of ideologically committed cadres—or perhaps ideologi-

---

of scale or government-created restrictions on entry have been more important in creating oligopolistic banking structures.

cal commitment by the bulk of the population—would also be crucial to the success of this kind of system. The system would require the daily allocation of scarce resources by thousands of government officials and managers. The temptation to allocate them toward family or friends, especially in the context of the low income levels of LDC's, could be great. A blend of basic honesty and fear of the consequences of getting caught is probably what keeps any economic system going. Ideological commitment, to supersede or at least temper motives of immediate personal gain, would provide the extra discipline that could prevent the private diversion of resources. Again, a good system of information, so that officials could check to see that decisions were being properly carried out and resources were not being diverted, would be necessary.

This kind of government-controlled system carries the potential for large, centrally directed mistakes.[4] But an attractive offset to this is the ability of the system to deal directly with the problems of income distribution and private economic power.

Some Realistic Policy Prescriptions

Few LDC's are likely to choose either "pure" system in next year's elections or next month's coup. No country has ever really embraced fully the competitive system I have described, and the practitioners of anything resembling the complete government control system are still few. Instead, most countries, LDC and developed alike, have a mixed system of private enterprise and government control. Some of the difficulties of this mixed system for LDC's have been described in general terms in Chap-

---

[4] Most observers have concluded that China's "Great Leap Forward" falls into this category.

ter 2, and the specific problems of Pakistan have been documented in this study. What does one recommend in the context of a mixed system?

It is important to realize that the economies of many LDC's may be primarily *private enterprise*, but they are certainly not *laissez faire*. The government is an active intervener in the economy, through its licensing, lending, and taxing powers. The government's ability to influence the allocation of resources and reward and penalize individuals through these measures may be as great as if it nationalizes most of the economy. This type of economy, then, represents active government intervention but private production and private appropriation of the benefits of the intervention. Petras, commenting on an economic and political structure in Chile that is similar in many respects to the one here described for Pakistan, has aptly labeled this kind of intervention as "socialism for the rich."[5] An important aspect of a mixed economy, then, is the degree to which the government is interventionist and creates barriers to entry, protected positions, and other favorable situations in which the benefits are privately appropriated by a small group.

In this context, policies that lean as far as possible away from government regulation and control and lean toward a competitive system ought to be pursued vigorously. The virtues of decentralized decision making appear to be very great, and the benefits of true competition are important. Removing the government-created barriers to entry, eliminating special protected positions, and generally encouraging competition are crucial steps. At the heart of any competitive system for LDC's, most of which have industrial sectors that are highly dependent on in-

[5] James Petras, *Politics and Social Forces in Chilean Development* (Berkeley, 1969), p. 50.

ternational trade, must be a relatively open international trade sector, with a realistic exchange rate, the absence of licensing, and modest tariffs.[6] Movements away from this competitive framework toward interventionism are very likely to lead to Petras' "socialism for the rich."

What about nationalization? There is no inherent reason why government operation of an industry should be less efficient than that of a private monopolist or a tight oligopoly. But the experience of many LDC's with nationalized industries has not been very favorable. In the context of a mixed system, private property, and generally low income, the opportunities for abuse, corruption, favoritism, and outright inefficiency appear to be great; one still, though, has to make some explicit welfare weightings and compare this to the private monopoly

[6] A number of East and Southeast Asian countries—notably Hong Kong, South Korea, Taiwan, and Singapore—have recently been successful in achieving rapid economic growth, good employment growth, and satisfactory distributions of income. Their successes have been, at least in part, attributable to their comparatively pro-competitive, open, outward-looking economic policies. There is no single good reference to these countries' policies and performances. Among the sources to look at are Ian Little, Tibor Scitovsky, and Maurice Scott, *Industry and Trade in Some Developing Countries*, ch. 7; Harry Oshima, "Labour Absorption in East and Southeast Asia," *Malayan Economic Review* (October 1971); David C. Cole and Princeton N. Lyman, *Korean Development; The Interplay of Politics and Economics* (Cambridge, Mass., 1971); Helen Hughes, "The Manufacturing Industry Sector," in *Southeast Asia's Economy in the 1970's*, Asian Development Bank (London, 1971); Helen Hughes, "The Scope for Labor Capital Substitution in the Developing Economies of Southeast and East Asia: A Sectoral Approach," Economic Staff Working Paper, No. 140, International Bank for Reconstruction and Development, Washington, D.C. (January 1973).

result before one can decide which is worse. But the strict dichotomy between private monopoly-oligopoly and nationalization is usually false. The monopoly-oligopoly position is frequently based on active government intervention in the economy. The best policy is always to remove that intervention. Again, for tradable goods this would mean primarily open-trade policies. Only in instances in which pro-competitive policies were not possible would I tend to favor nationalization.

Miracles cannot be expected from income distribution in a low income LDC like Pakistan. The surplus to be gained from effective taxation of the rich can raise somewhat the incomes of those at the very bottom, but the figures indicating an average per capita income of Rs. 500-600 for Pakistan mean just that. The best use of this surplus would probably be in the schooling-health-medical areas, with special efforts to insure that these expenditures reached the bulk of the agricultural population, rather than being appropriated exclusively by the urban middle class. In effect, this would be substituting the formation of human and social overhead capital that would be owned on a much wider basis in place of part of the formation of physical capital which would have been owned by a narrow few.

Pakistan's Policies

Prior to 1969, only weak efforts were made to decrease industrial concentration in Pakistan. There were no specific remedial policies with respect to concentration by industry, and, as we have seen, the import licensing system tended to exacerbate the effects of concentration. The income tax was not used as a weapon to combat the economy-wide concentration that had developed. The only relevant policies that affected economy-wide concen-tration were those pertaining to corporate taxes and the stock market.

As part of an effort to encourage private saving and channel it toward the industrial sector, the government tried to widen the base of ownership of industrial assets by encouraging private corporations to make their shares available to the public. Companies that went public paid taxes at a lower rate than privately held companies. Fur-ther, in 1963, the government considered applying the tax break only to those companies in which over 50% of the shares were held by 20 persons or more. Since most publicly listed companies would not have qualified at the time, the industrial and financial community objected and the government withdrew the provision. After pro-crastinating for five years, the government, in 1968, finally decided to apply the 50% rule only to newly floated companies.

Since the government believed that investors were dis-trustful of the manipulations of the managers of com-panies and strongly preferred to receive dividends rather than take their chances on reinvested profits and capital gains, it offered a tax break on profits that were distrib-uted as dividends. Since this by itself did not seem to en-courage enough dividends, a tax penalty was levied on firms whose retained earnings ("surplus" or "reserves") exceeded their equity capital. Firms soon learned to evade this by capitalizing their retained earnings through the use of "bonus shares" (stock dividends), and the gov-ernment responded with a tax on the issuance of bonus shares.

To further encourage investors to devote their savings to acquiring industrial assets, the government formed a mutual fund, the National Investment (Unit) Trust

(NIT) in 1963, and followed with the formation of the Investment Corporation of Pakistan (ICP) in 1966, which subsequently floated mutual funds, acted as a stockbroker for small investors, undertook major underwriting efforts for new issues, and generally bought stock on the market to support the stock market. The government's initial investment in ICP was Rs.100 million; by 1970, an extra Rs.130 million had been allocated to ICP.

The success of the government policies in attracting new investors to the stock market and diversifying industrial ownership is difficult to measure. By 1969, the NIT and ICP mutual funds together constituted about 10% of the value of traded shares. Another 2%-3% was in the ICP portfolio from underwriting and straight purchases. Banks and insurance companies owned about 20% of the value of traded shares, but many of these were controlled by the large industrial families. The bulk of the remainder was still in the hands of the controlling families and groups. It is unlikely that the percentage of outstanding shares held by the general public was much above the 5% figure that it had been in the early 1960's. The ambitious ICP scheme for attracting individual investors and providing them with investment advice and margin loans had netted only Rs.6.3 million in investments by 1970, far less than 1% of the value of traded shares.

In the end, though, these efforts really could not have affected the control position of the large industrial families, since even a sizeable minority position would have been sufficient for control. Further, the families' wealth could only be increased by efforts to buoy up the stock market through direct or indirect means. The only action that might have diversified stock ownership and reduced the wealth of the large families—the effort to force listed companies to expand their number of shareholders—was rescinded when it caused a severe fall in stock prices. In short, these policies of the 1960's may have diversified industrial wealth slightly, but they certainly did not impair the positions of the large industrial families and groups and surely added to their wealth.

In 1969, in the wake of the disorders that had brought down the Ayub Khan government and amid rising concern about the concentration of industrial power, a monopoly control ordinance was proposed, and in February 1970 the Monopolies and Restrictive Trade Practices (Control and Prevention) Ordinance of 1970 was promulgated. The ordinance was aimed at economic power in the large, monopoly power in individual industries, and restrictive practices within industries.[7]

The ordinance established a Monopoly Control Authority (MCA) to administer the ordinance and to register companies and agreements that might be subject to its provisions. This registration function is similar to that found in the British Restrictive Practices Act of 1956. The basic idea is that there generally are no per se illegal practices or structures. Rather, all practices, agreements, and dominant market situations have to be registered with the MCA, which then investigates each one to see if it is in the public interest or if it should be dissolved.

The MCA has jurisdiction over situations of "undue economic power." This is defined as a company with Rs.10 million that has not gone public, a company with Rs.10 million in assets that is 50% or more owned by

[7] For a more extended discussion of the ordinance than is contained here, see B. J. Linder and Asit Sarkar, "Pakistan's Monopolies and Restrictive Practices Ordinance," *The Antitrust Bulletin* (Fall 1971).

an individual or his close family, and any dealings between two or more "associated companies"[8] that preju-
dice the interests of the shareholders of some of the companies. This last provision is aimed at a managing agency
or a buying or selling agency relationship in which an
agency could milk the company, to the detriment of the
latter's minority stockholders. The ordinance gives the
MCA the power to require firms with over Rs.10 million
in assets to go public, to require owners of more than
50% of the shares of a company to sell some of their
shares, and to regulate dealings between associated companies.

"Monopoly power" also comes under the jurisdiction
of the MCA. This is defined by the ordinance as the
"ability of one or more sellers in a market to set non-
competitive prices or restrict output without losing a
substantial share of the market or to exclude others from
any part of that market." But only "unreasonable monopoly power" is prohibited, and this is defined to cover a
situation in which two or more associated companies control 20% or more of a market, a merger that would
create monopoly power or substantially lessen competition, or a loan from a bank or insurance company to an
associated company on terms more favorable than for
loans to other companies in comparable situations. Market power per se is not defined as unreasonable monopoly
power. The MCA can require divestiture or dissolution
of the offending companies. It can also regulate bank
and insurance company loans and investments in these
offending situations. An effective defense in the above

[8] "Associated companies" were defined by the ordinance as
companies in which someone who was an owner, partner, officer,
or director, or who owned 20% of the shares of one company
was also an owner, partner, etc. of another.

three situations is that the action yielded efficiency, technological progress, or the promotion of exports and that these benefits could not be gained by means that were less restrictive of competition and that they more than outweighted the adverse effects of the lessening of competition.

Finally, the MCA also has power over "unreasonably restrictive trade practices," which are defined as price fixing, market sharing, collective refusals to deal, tying arrangements, and resale price maintenance. The MCA can prohibit these practices. Again, efficiency, technological progress, and exports are a defense.

The ordinance represents an ambitious effort on the part of the government to come to grips with the problems of industrial concentration, while retaining the basic structure and spirit of the Pakistani economic system. The ordinance is designed to weaken the economic power of the large industrial families and groups, but not destroy it. Only a confiscatory tax could do that. The problem of the price at which the families would have to disinvest excessive shareholdings has been solved by the ordinance as follows: they can expect at least a minimum price halfway between the original issue price of the shares and their net worth. If the general public does not want to buy at that price, no further disinvestment can be required for at least three years.

The monopoly power and restrictive practices provisions of the ordinance are almost as strong as one could hope, with the exception of the absence of a per se market power prohibition. The Monopoly Control Authority has plenty of room to define markets as broadly or narrowly as it wishes. But the ordinance could not get at the heart of the most important barriers to entry: the restrictive import licensing system. Import licensing was simply outside the authority of the ordinance.

Though the ordinance was promulgated in February 1970, the members of the Monopoly Control Authority were not appointed until August 1971, and the Authority did not begin officially exercising its powers until January 1972. Thus, the monopoly control ordinance has not yet had an opportunity to have an effect on the economy. It will be truly interesting to see if Pakistan's legal traditions will be able to absorb and deal effectively with the ordinance and if sufficient political will within Pakistan exists to make it work.

In December 1971, in the aftermath of Pakistan's military defeat by India and the loss of Bangladesh, Z. A. Bhutto came to power as the new president of Pakistan. He and his political party had earlier campaigned for the national assembly on a reformist platform, promising to redistribute income and land and to curb the economic power of the large industrial families.

In January 1972 the government "nationalized" the 31 large firms in 10 industries: iron and steel; basic metals; heavy engineering; heavy electrical equipment; motor vehicles; tractors; petrochemical industries; gas and oil refineries; cement; and electricity. Government firms were already the dominant producers in heavy engineering, heavy electrical equipment, petrochemicals, and cement. Of the 31 firms that were "nationalized," 22 were controlled by the leading families and groups analyzed in this study. The textile, sugar, paper, vegetable ghee, and other consumer goods industries were left untouched. In March 1972, the life insurance industry was similarly "nationalized."

The "nationalization" consisted of the government's

appointing managers to run the companies, while allowing the former owners to retain nominal ownership of their assets. One of the primary goals of this measure seemed simply to achieve greater honesty in the reporting of corporate profits and the payment of taxes. As of this writing, the real focus of control and power in these companies is unclear.[9] When the Karachi Stock Exchange reopened in May 1972, the share prices of these "nationalized" firms did not decline precipitously, which indicated that their owners did not try to dump their shares on the market. Either the owners presently feel themselves in effective control or have high enough hopes of regaining control.

Other reformist actions were taken during the same period. The government promulgated an ordinance requiring pharmaceuticals to be sold by their generic names.[10] Simultaneously with the "nationalization" of the industrial firms, the institution of the managing agency was abolished for all firms, and the power of minority stockholders to elect company directors was strengthened.[11] In May, the government increased its supervisory powers over bank dealings with firms in which there was some joint interest.

Most importantly, in May 1972 the rupee was devalued from Rs.4.76 = $1 to Rs.11.00 = $1. Simultaneously, the licensing system was dropped, the bonus voucher

[9] Foreign-controlled insurance companies, though, have been effectively nationalized and their former owners have been offered compensation.

[10] This seems to be another case of the special concern of the middle class strongly influencing government policy.

[11] The holder of each share was entitled to cast as many votes as there were directors to be elected, but he could cast them all for one director if he chose. Hence, a minority, by concentrating its votes, could more easily elect one or more directors.

system was scrapped, and import duties were scaled down. The intention of the government was to open up the import system to competition and thereby open up the economy to competition. Under the new foreign exchange system, capital goods worth up to Rs.200,000 are importable without licenses and capital goods worth Rs.200,000 to Rs.500,000 are importable without licenses if they are obtained on barter or credit terms. Capital goods over Rs.500,000 will still be open to scrutiny. Raw materials are largely importable without licenses, though some imports are restricted to tied aid or barter sources. Also, the Trading Corporation of Pakistan (the government export-import company) retains its import monopoly over a few crucial items like pig iron and steel billets. Some consumer goods can be imported without licenses, but the bans on the import of a number of domestically produced consumer goods are still in effect, as are moderate import tariffs. Raw materials exports are subject to substantial export taxes (40% on raw cotton), providing substantial subsidies to domestic manufacturers using those raw materials.

Overall, the new foreign exchange system represents a substantial unwinding of the direct controls of the previous twenty years. The new system is not wholly free of distortions, but few foreign exchange systems are, in less developed and developed countries alike. One can only hope that when strains develop on the system, as is almost inevitable, the government will stick by its commitment to the new system and use exchange rate adjustments to deal with balance-of-payments difficulties rather than slide back into a system of direct controls.

Taxation has been the new government's weakest area. Still needed for Pakistan, both as an added curb on economic power and for straightforward income redistribution, is an effective, progressive taxation system. On balance, though, the policies of Pakistan's new government have gone a long way toward opening up the economy and making it more competitive. Many of the biases in the economy toward capital-intensive production have been diminished, and the processes of labor absorption should accelerate. If the new government can solve its domestic and international political problems and maintain a set of outward-looking, pro-competitive economic policies, Pakistan may again become a success story among the LDC's.

Appendix to Chapter 4

A. Estimating the Assets of Unlisted Companies Owned by the 43 Leading Families and Groups

THE assets of the unlisted companies owned or controlled by the 43 leading families and groups were estimated in two major ways. First, if anything was known about the physical characteristics of a firm (e.g., the number of spindles and looms in a textile factory or the tonnage capacity of a sugar factory), this firm was matched with a firm of similar characteristics listed on the Karachi Stock Exchange and for which, therefore, total assets were readily available. These characteristics were derived from industry yearbooks and special studies. It was assumed that the assets of the former firm would be roughly the same as those of the latter.

For cotton textiles, the data were good enough and plentiful enough that simple regression analysis could be used to aid this "fitting" process. There were 38 cotton textile firms whose assets were listed on the Karachi Stock Exchange and for which the numbers of spindles and looms were available. Using ordinary least squares, I fitted an equation of the following form (the numbers in parentheses are t-statistics):

$$A = 0.21 + 0.95\,S + 0.87\,L + 2.78\,D$$
$$(0.04)\ (4.26)\quad (0.83)\quad (0.53)$$
$$R^2 = 0.72$$

where A is the book value of total assets in millions of rupees (average: Rs.26.5 million), S is the number of spindles in thousands (average: 24.5 thousand), L is the number of looms in hundreds (average: 2.2 hundred), and D is a 0,1 dummy variable indicating the absence or presence of dying and finishing equipment. The coefficients of this equation are reasonable, and the overall fit is good. This equation was then used to estimate the assets of unlisted cotton textile firms, since in all cases the numbers of spindles and looms for these firms was available.

In cases in which the physical characteristics of firms were unknown, I used estimates of the net worth of these companies that were made by individuals close to Karachi business circles. To expand these net worth estimates up to total assets, I used the following estimated relationship, derived from a sample of 68 listed firms of the leading families (the numbers in parentheses are t-statistics):

$$\log A = 1.13 + 0.93 \log NW$$
$$(6.08)(26.27)$$
$$R^2 = 0.91$$

where A is total assets and NW is net worth. This seems to be a reasonable relationship, since it is consistent with the hypothesis that larger firms are better able to attract non-equity financing and have less need to rely on self-finance. Also, information from investment sanctioning records was used as a general check on the overall size of a firm.

B. Estimating the Assets of Companies Listed
   Exclusively on the Dacca Stock Exchange

Estimates for the assets of the 36 firms listed exclusively on the Dacca Stock Exchange came from a number of sources. For firms controlled by the East Pakistan Industrial Development Corporation, the 1967 assets are available from the 1966-1967 EPIDC Annual Report (but, curiously, the 1968 assets are not available from the 1967-1968 annual report). These were expanded by an 8% growth factor to bring them up to 1968. The assets of other firms for 1966 were available from the *Stock Exchange Guide of Pakistan*, and these were expanded by 16.6% to bring them up to 1968.[1] Still other firms were matched with firms of known assets and similar characteristics, as described in the previous section.

The estimated total assets for these 36 firms came to Rs.1.267.9 million, of which Rs.603.6 million were accounted for by EPIDC firms.

C. Estimating the Total Assets of Foreign-Controlled Manufacturing Firms

We know that the 11 foreign-controlled manufacturing firms listed on the Karachi Stock Exchange had total assets of Rs.887.7 million in 1968. But there were many other foreign-controlled firms not listed, and we must estimate the assets for all foreign-controlled manufacturing firms in 1968.

The State Bank of Pakistan provides an estimate of the net asset position of foreign-controlled manufacturing companies for 1968.[2] Our effort must be to expand these figures to total assets. The figures are divided into those

[1] Iqbal Haidari and Abdul Hafeez Khan, *Stock Exchange Guide of Pakistan*, rev. ed. (Karachi, 1968).

[2] The "net asset" position consists of the equity owned by foreigners in firms in Pakistan and the debt owed by these firms to foreigners. See State Bank of Pakistan, *Foreign Liabilities and Assets and Foreign Investments in Pakistan, 1967-69* (Karachi, 1971).

for firms incorporated abroad (but doing manufacturing business in Pakistan) and those incorporated in Pakistan in which foreigners held a 25% or greater interest.

The firms incorporated abroad had net assets of Rs. 74.4 million. These firms were wholly owned by foreigners, so there are no problems of minority Pakistani ownership. These figures should be expanded by roughly 45% (the amount by which total assets exceeded net worth for foreign firms listed on the Karachi Exchange) to Rs. 107.9 million in total assets.

The process is somewhat more complicated for the manufacturing firms incorporated in Pakistan. These companies had Rs.488.8 million in net worth that was owned abroad.[3] This was roughly 70% of the overall net worth of these firms, allowing for minority Pakistani shareholdings. The overall net worth of the companies, then, was Rs.698.3 million. If we expand this by 45%, we get Rs.1,012.5 million in total assets for these firms. The total assets, then, for all foreign-controlled manu-

[3] This figure was derived as follows: The State Bank figures show long-term obligations (equity and debt) of the companies with 25% or more foreign ownership at Rs.627.1 million. The figures also show the equity holdings of foreigners in all manufacturing corporations (including those with less than 25% foreign ownership) at Rs.530.0 million, and the long-term debt to foreigners by all manufacturing corporations at Rs.189.4 million. Since 27% of short-term debt over the 1967-1969 period was owed by the companies with less than 25% foreign ownership, I assumed that this percentage held true for long-term debt as well. This meant that Rs.51.1 million in long-term debt was owed by these companies and Rs.138.3 million was owed by the corporations with over 25% foreign ownership. Subtracting this Rs.138.3 million from the Rs.627.1 million long-term obligation of these foreign-controlled companies leaves Rs.488.8 million in net worth.

facturing firms was the sum of this figure and the figure for firms incorporated abroad, or Rs.1,120.4 million.

D. Estimating All Manufacturing Assets in Pakistan

There is no good estimate of all manufacturing assets available for Pakistan. The only measure that attempts to cover all "large-scale" manufacturing is the estimate for the value of fixed assets presented in the East and West Pakistan Censuses of Manufacturing Industries. "Large-scale" includes all those firms employing 20 or more workers or using power. These figures, though, are underestimates of the total assets involved in manufacturing, for two reasons: they neglect current assets (cash, accounts receivable, and inventories) and they appear systematically to report lower levels of fixed assets than are reported in comparable balance sheet compilations. Since consistency is necessary to allow comparisons between the estimated assets for the 43 leading families and the estimated assets for all manufacturing, the method of expanding the CMI figures should be consistent with the balance sheet concepts used for the former estimates.

The method used here was as follows: For each of 6 identifiable industries in West Pakistan, balance sheet assets were available for a number of firms listed on the Karachi Stock Exchange, along with physical capacity estimates for these firms. Estimates for the total physical capacity in these industries at mid-1968 were also available. Using the ratio of total capacity to the capacity of the listed firms, we expanded the assets of the listed firms to an estimate of the total assets in the industry. For a seventh industry, cotton textiles, the equation described in section A on estimating the unlisted assets of the 43 families was used. The numbers of firms, spindles, looms, and finishing facilities in the industry were plugged into the equation, and an estimate for the total assets in the industry was achieved.

The sum of the estimated total assets for these 7 industries was then compared to the sum for these industries reported by the CMI,[4] and this ratio was used to expand the total for fixed assets in all manufacturing reported by the CMI. The resulting estimate for the total assets of all "large-scale" manufacturing in West Pakistan is Rs.9,477.2 million. These figures are summarized in Table 4A-1.

A similar procedure was applied to 2 industries plus cotton textiles for East Pakistan.[5] The estimated total for all of Pakistan is Rs.15,059.0 million. This figure, unfortunately, excludes small-scale and cottage manufacturing, but there are no good estimates of the size or extent of small-scale and cottage manufacturing. The national accounts estimate for this sector has simply expanded this sector by the estimated rate of population growth from an initial guessing point.

For purposes of calculating concentration figures, we also need to be able to subtract foreign-controlled and government-controlled assets. The foreign-controlled assets have already been estimated in the previous section. The assets of government-controlled firms were estimated in the following manner: these firms were primarily under the control of the East and West Pakistan Industrial Development Corporations. Four firms with assets of Rs.407.2 million were listed on the Karachi Stock Exchange. The 1966-1967 EPIDC Annual Report listed an additional 17 firms or projects that were in production

---

[4] These 7 industries accounted for 46% of the assets reported in the West Pakistan CMI.

[5] These 3 industries accounted for 46% of the assets reported in the East Pakistan CMI.

Estimates of Total Assets in Manufacturing, 1968

	Capacity of Sample Firms (1)	Assets of Sample Firms (Rs. millions) (2)	Total Capacity in Industry (3)	Estimated Total Assets in Industry (Rs. millions) (4)	Fixed Assets Reported by CMI (Rs. millions) (5)
West Pakistan					
Cotton textiles[a]	25,260 spindles	Rs.78.9	56,173 spindles	Rs.2,340.0	Rs.882.9
Wool textiles	20,440 tons/day	515.0	25,500 tons/day	175.5	53.7
Sugar	37,360 tons/year	77.6	120,680 tons/year	642.5	388.0
Vegetable ghee	17,574 million/year	221.0	20,578 million/year	250.7	81.0
Cigarettes				258.8	51.3
Jute	519 looms	122.6	519 looms	122.6	96.8
Cement	2,300 million tons/year	408.6	3,140 million tons/year	557.8	190.1
Total				Rs.4,347.9	Rs.1,743.8
Ratio of column (4) to (5)				2.49	
Fixed assets for all manufacturing reported by CMI					Rs.3,806.1
Estimated total assets for all manufacturing				Rs.9,477.2	
East Pakistan					
Cotton textiles[a]	9,950 looms	Rs.833.8	17,614 looms	Rs.715.0	Rs.244.4
Jute				1,476.0	564.5
Sugar	94,106 tons/year	320.7	109,400 tons/year	372.8	120.5
Total				Rs.2,563.8	Rs.929.4
Ratio of column (4) to (5)				2.76	
Fixed assets for all manufacturing reported by CMI					Rs.2,022.4
Estimated total assets for all manufacturing				Rs.5,581.8	

[a] See text for description of cotton textile estimate.

SOURCES: Government of West Pakistan, *Directory of Industrial Establishments in West Pakistan* (Lahore, 1969); Saeed Hafeez, *Industrial Reference Guide* (Karachi, 1969); Saeed Hafeez, *Textile Yearbook* (Karachi, 1970); *Directory of Pakistan Cotton Textile Industry* (Karachi, 1970); Mansur Ahmad, "Vegetable Ghee Industry in West Pakistan," Directorate of Industries and Commerce, Government of West Pakistan (Lahore, 1969); K. S. Hassan, "Cigarette Manufacturing Industry in West Pakistan," Directorate of Industries and Commerce, Government of West Pakistan (Lahore, 1969).

(or that subsequently came into production in 1967-1968), with total assets of Rs.1.381.3 million. An 8% growth factor brings this to Rs.1,491.8 million. The 1968-1969 WPIDC Annual Report listed an additional 15 manufacturing firms under its control. Unfortunately, the balance sheets for these firms are not provided for these firms, but by matching characteristics, I have estimated the assets of these firms at Rs.823.0 million. Finally, the West Pakistan Department of Industries operated 2 cement factories, worth roughly Rs.72 million. The total for all government-controlled firms comes to Rs. 2,794.0 million.

Bibliography

Books

Bain, Joe S., *Barriers to New Competition*, Cambridge, Mass.: Harvard University Press, 1956.

————, *Industrial Organization*, 2nd edn., New York: Wiley, 1968.

————, *International Differences in Industrial Structure*, New Haven: Yale University Press, 1966.

Berle, Adolf, and Means, Gardiner, *The Modern Corporation and Private Property*, New York: Macmillan, 1932.

Brandenburg, Frank, *The Development of Latin American Private Enterprise*, Planning Pamphlet No. 121, Washington, D.C.: National Planning Association, 1964.

Caves, Richard E., *American Industry: Structure, Behavior, Performance*, 3rd edn., Englewood Cliffs: Prentice-Hall, 1972.

Chamberlin, Edward H., *The Theory of Monopolistic Competition*, 8th edn., Cambridge, Mass.: Harvard University Press, 1962.

Cole, David C., and Lyman, Princeton N., *Korean Development; the Interplay of Politics and Economics*, Cambridge, Mass.: Harvard University Press, 1971.

Domhoff, G. William, *The Higher Circles*, New York: Random House, 1970.

Domhoff, G. William, *Who Rules America?* Englewood Cliffs: Prentice-Hall, 1967.

Fellner, William, *Competition Among the Few*, New York: Knopf, 1949.

Fillol, Tomás Roberto, *Social Factors in Economic Development: The Argentine Case*, Cambridge: MIT Press, 1961.

Florence, P. Sargant, *Ownership, Control and Success of Large Companies*, London: Sweet & Maxwell, 1961.

Galbraith, John Kenneth, *The New Industrial State*, Boston: Houghton Mifflin, 1967.

Hazari, E. K., *The Corporate Private Sector*, Bombay: Asia Publishing House, 1966.

Hsing, Mo-Huan; Power, John H.; and Sicat, Gerardo P., *Taiwan and the Philippines: Industrialization and Trade Policies*, London: Oxford University Press, 1970.

Jewkes, John; Sawyers, David; and Stillerman, Richard, *The Sources of Invention*, 2nd edn., New York: Norton, 1969.

Kothari, M. L., *Industrial Combinations*, Allahabad: Chaitanya Publishing House, 1967.

Lagos, Ricardo, *La Concentracion del Poder Economico*, Santiago: Editorial del Pacifico, 1962.

Lewis, Stephen R., Jr., *Economic Policy and Industrial Growth in Pakistan*, London: George Allen & Unwin, 1969.

————, *Pakistan: Industrialization and Trade Policies*, London: Oxford University Press, 1970.

Little, Ian; Scitovsky, Tibor; and Scott, Maurice, *Industry and Trade in Some Developing Countries*, London: Oxford University Press, 1970.

Malpica, Carlos, *Los Dueños del Peru*, 3rd edn., Lima: Ediciones Ensayos Sociales, 1968.

Mason, Edward S., ed., *The Corporation and Modern Society*, Cambridge, Mass.: Harvard University Press, 1959.

Merhav, Meir, *Technological Dependence, Monopoly, and Growth*, New York: Pergamon Press, 1969.

Mills, C. Wright, *The Power Elite*, New York: Oxford University Press, 1956.

Mintz, Morton, and Cohen, Jerry S., *America, Inc.*, New York: Dial, 1971.

National Christian Council of Kenya, *Who Owns Kenya?* Nairobi: 1968

Papanek, Gustav F., *Pakistan's Development: Social Goals and Private Incentives*, Cambridge: Harvard University Press, 1967.

Petras, James, *Politics and Social Forces in Chilean Development*, Berkeley: University of California Press, 1969.

Phlips, Louis, *Effects of Industrial Concentration: A Cross-Section Analysis for the Common Market*, Amsterdam: North-Holland Publishing Company, 1971.

Safarian, A. E., *Foreign Ownership of Canadian Industry*, Toronto: McGraw-Hill, 1966.

Scherer, F. M., *Industrial Market Structure and Economic Performance*, Chicago: Rand McNally, 1970.

Warner, W. Lloyd; Unwala, Darab, B.; and Trimm, John H., *The Emergent American Society*, Vol. I, New Haven: Yale University Press, 1967.

Wheelwright, E. L. and Miskelly, J., *Anatomy of Australian Manufacturing Industry*, Sydney: The Law Book Company, 1967.

White, Lawrence J., *The Automobile Industry Since 1945*, Cambridge, Mass.: Harvard University Press, 1971.

Compendia on Pakistan Trade, Industry, and
Stock Market

M. M. Ansari, ed., *Ansari's Trade and Industrial Direc-
tory*, 9th ed., Karachi: 1966.
A. M. Barque, ed., *Barque's Pakistan Trade Directory*,
Karachi: 1964.
————, ed., *Who's Who in Pakistan*, 1962-1963. La-
hore: Barque & Co., 1963.
Federation of Pakistan Chambers of Commerce and In-
dustry, *Directory of Pakistan Commerce and Industry*,
Karachi: 1969.
Hafeez, Saeed, *Industrial Reference Guide*, Karachi:
Press Corporation of Pakistan, 1969.
————, *Textile Year Book*, Karachi: Press Corporation
of Pakistan, 1970.
Haidari, Iqbal, and Khan, Abdul Hafeez, *Stock Ex-
change Guide of Pakistan*, rev. edn., Karachi: Eco-
nomic and Industrial Publication, 1968.
Karachi Stock Exchange, *Year Book*, Karachi: 1968.
Khan, Khan Takawas Ali, ed., *Biographical Encyclo-
pedia of Pakistan*, 1969-1970, Lahore: 1970.
Tareen, Ameen K., ed., *Directory of Pakistan Cotton
Textile Industry*, Karachi: 1970.

Pakistan Periodicals

Business Recorder (Karachi, daily)
Daily Business Post (Karachi, daily)
Dawn (Karachi, daily)
Finance and Industry (Karachi, monthly)
Pakistan Times (Lahore and Rawalpindi, daily)

Articles and Monographs

Adams, Walter, and Dirlam, Joel B., "Big Steel, Inven-

Bibliography

tion, and Innovation," *Quarterly Journal of Economics*, Vol. LXXX, No. 2 (May 1966).

Adelman, Morris A., "Comment on the 'H' Concentration Measure as a Numbers-Equivalent," *Review of Economics and Statistics*, Vol. LI, No. 1 (February 1969).

———, "Monopoly and Concentration: Comparisons in Time and Space," *Revista Internazionale di Scienze Economiche e Commerciali*, Vol. XII, No. 8 (August 1965).

Ahmad, Mansur, "Vegetable Ghee Industry in West Pakistan," Directorate of Industries and Commerce, Government of West Pakistan (Lahore: 1969).

Alamgir, Mohiuddin, "The Domestic Prices of Imported Commodities in Pakistan: A Further Study," *Pakistan Development Review*, Vol. VIII, No. 1 (Spring 1968).

Arndt, Helmut, Testimony in *Economic Concentration*, Part 7, hearings before the Subcommittee on Antitrust and Monopoly, Committee on the Judiciary, U.S. Senate, Washington, D.C.: 1968.

Bergan, Asbjorn, "Personal Income Distribution and Personal Savings in Pakistan, 1963/64," *Pakistan Development Review*, Vol. VII, No. 2 (Summer 1967).

Business Week, "The 'Wallenberg Boys'—and How They Grew," February 25, 1967.

Chaudhry, Shahid Amjad, "Private Foreign Investment in Pakistan," *Pakistan Development Review*, Vol. X, No. 1 (Spring 1970).

Chelliah, Raja J. "Trends in Taxation in Developing Countries," *IMF Staff Papers*, Vol. XVIII, No. 2 (July 1971).

Child, Frank C., "Liberalization of the Foreign Exchange Market," *Pakistan Development Review*, Vol. VIII, No. 2 (Summer 1968).

Child, Frank C., "Reform of a Trade and Payments System: The Case of Pakistan," *Economic Development and Cultural Change*, Vol. XVI, No. 4 (July 1968).

Chow, Gregory C., "Tests of Equality Between Sets of Coefficients in Two Linear Regressions," *Econometrica*, Vol. XXVIII, No. 3 (July 1960).

Corden, William M., "The Structure of a Tariff System and the Effective Protection Rate," *Journal of Political Economy*, Vol. LXXIV, No. 3 (June 1966).

Diaz-Alejandro, Carlos F., "The Mechanisms for Containing Imports: The System During 1972 and a Retrospective Look at its Evolution (Import Controls)," Center Discussion Paper No. 158, Yale University Economic Growth Center (September 1972).

Dooley, Peter C. "The Interlocking Directorate," *American Economic Review*, Vol. LIX, No. 3 (June 1969).

Esposito, Louis, and Esposito, Frances Ferguson, "Foreign Competition and Domestic Industry Profitability," *Review of Economics and Statistics*, Vol. LIII, No. 4 (November 1971).

Fortune, Vol. LXXI, No. 5 (May 1970); Vol. LXXI, No. 6 (June 1970); Vol. LXXII, No. 2 (August 1970).

Fulda, Carl H., and Till, Irene, "Concentration and Competitive Potential in India," *The Antitrust Bulletin*, Vol. XIII (Fall 1968).

Glassburner, Bruce, "Aspects of the Problem of Foreign Exchange Pricing in Pakistan," *Economic Development and Cultural Change*, Vol. XVI, No. 4 (July 1968).

Griffen, Keith B., "Financing Development Plans in Pakistan," *Pakistan Development Review*, Vol. V, No. 4 (Winter 1965).

————, and Glassburner, Bruce, "An Evaluation of Pakistan's Third Five Year Plan," *Journal of Development Studies*, Vol. II, No. 4 (July 1966).

Guisinger, Stephen E., "Negative Value Added and the Theory of Effective Protection," *Quarterly Journal of Economics*, Vol. LXXXIII, No. 3 (August 1969).

Haq, Khadija, and Baqai, Moin, "Savings and Financial Flows in the Corporate Sector, 1959-63," *Pakistan Development Review*, Vol. VII, No. 3 (Autumn 1967).

Hassan, K. S., "Cigarette Manufacturing Industry in West Pakistan," Directorate of Industries and Commerce, Government of West Pakistan (Lahore: 1969).

Hogan, Warren P., "Capacity Creation and Utilization in Pakistan Manufacturing Industry," *Australian Economic Papers*, Vol. VII, No. 10 (June 1968).

Hufbauer, Gary C., "West Pakistan Exports: Effective Taxation, Policy Promotion, and Sectoral Discrimination," in *Development Policy: The Pakistan Experience*, W. P. Falcon and G. F. Papanek, eds., Cambridge, Mass.: Harvard University Press, 1971.

Hughes, Helen, "The Manufacturing Industry Sector," in *Southeast Asia Economy in the 1970's*, Asian Development Bank, London: Longmans, 1971.

————, "The Scope for Labor Capital Substitution in the Developing Economies of Southeast and East Asia: A Sectoral Approach," Economic Staff Working Paper No. 140, International Bank for Reconstruction and Development, Washington, D.C. (January 1973).

Hunt, Shane, "Distribution, Growth, and Government Economic Behavior in Peru," in *Government and Economic Development*, Gustav Ranis, ed., New Haven: Yale University Press, 1971.

Islam, A. I. Aminul, "An Estimation of the Extent of Overvaluation of the Domestic Currency in Pakistan at the Official Rate of Exchange, 1948/49-1964/65,"

Pakistan Development Review, Vol. x, No. 1 (Spring 1970).

Islam, Nurul, "Exchange Control, Liberalization, and Economic Growth in Pakistan," mimeo, 1971.

Khan, Amir U., and Duff, Bart, "Development of Agricultural Mechanization Technologies of the International Rice Research Institute," Paper No. 72-02, Agricultural Engineering Department, International Rice Research Institute (January 1973).

Khan, Azizur Rahman, "Capital-Intensity and the Efficiency of Factor Use: A Comparative Study of the Observed Capital-Labour Ratios of Pakistani Industries," *Pakistan Development Review*, Vol. x, No. 2 (Summer 1970).

Killick, Anthony J., "Price Controls, Inflation, and Income Distribution: The Ghanaian Experience," mimeo, presented at the Torremolinos Conference of the Development Advisory Service of Harvard University (September 1972).

Larner, Robert J., "Ownership and Control in the 200 Largest Nonfinancial Corporations, 1929 and 1963," *American Economics Review*, Vol. LVI, No. 4 (September 1966).

Leibenstein, Harvey, "Allocative Efficiency vs. X-Efficiency," *American Economic Review*, Vol. LVI, No. 3 (June 1966).

Lewis, Stephen R., Jr., "The Effects of Trade Policy on Domestic Relative Prices: Pakistan, 1951-65," *American Economics Review*, Vol. LVIII, No. 1 (March 1968).

———, and Guisinger, Stephen E., "Measuring Protection in a Developing Country: The Case of Pakistan," *Journal of Political Economy*, Vol. LXXVI, No. 6 (December 1968).

————, "The Structure of Protection in Pakistan," in *The Structure of Protection in Developing Countries,* Bela Balassa, ed., Baltimore: Johns Hopkins Press, 1971.

Lewis, W. Arthur, "Economic Development with Unlimited Supply of Labour," *The Manchester School,* Vol. xxii, No. 2 (May 1954).

Linder, B. J., and Sarkar, Asit, "Pakistan's Monopolies and Restrictive Practices Ordinance," *The Antitrust Bulletin,* Vol. xvi, No. 3 (Fall 1971).

Lipsey, R. G., and Lancaster, K., "The General Theory of Second Best," *Review of Economic Studies,* Vol. xxiv, No. 63 (1956-1957).

Miller, John Perry, "Measures of Monopoly Power and Concentration: Their Economic Significance," in *Business Concentration and Price Policy,* National Bureau of Economic Research, Princeton: Princeton University Press, 1955.

Naqvi, S. N. H., "Import Licensing in Pakistan," *Pakistan Development Review,* Vol. iv, No. 1 (Spring 1964).

Oshima, Harry, "Labour Absorption in East and Southeast Asia," *Malayan Economic Review,* Vol. xvi, No. 2 (October 1971).

Pal, Mati Lal, "The Determinants of the Domestic Price of Imports," *Pakistan Development Review,* Vol. iv, No. 4 (Winter 1964).

————, "Domestic Prices of Imports in Pakistan, Extension of Empirical Findings," *Pakistan Development Review,* Vol. v, No. 4 (Winter 1965).

Papanek, Gustav F., "The Development of Entrepreneurship," *American Economic Review,* Vol. lii, No. 2 (May 1962).

————, "The Industrial Entrepreneurs—Education, Occupational Background and Finance," in *Development Policy: The Pakistan Experience*, W. P. Falcon and G. F. Papanek, eds., Cambridge, Mass.: Harvard University Press, 1971.

Papanek, Hannah, "Pakistan's Big Businessmen: Muslim Separation, Entrepreneurship and Partial Modernization," *Economic Development and Cultural Change*, Vol. XXI, No. 1 (October 1972).

Power, John H., "Industrialization in Pakistan: A Case of Frustrated Take-Off?" *Pakistan Development Review*, Vol. III, No. 2 (Summer 1963).

Pryor, Frederick L., "An International Comparison of Concentration Ratios," *Review of Economics and Statistics*, Vol. LIV, No. 2 (May 1972).

Rab, Abdur, *Income Taxation in Pakistan*, unpublished Ph.D. thesis (Harvard University, 1968).

Radhu, G. M. "The Rate Structure of Indirect Taxes in Pakistan," *Pakistan Development Review*, Vol. IV, No. 3 (Autumn 1964).

Ranis, Gustav, "Review of Books by Lewis and Mac-Ewan," *Journal of International Economics*, Vol. 2, No. 2 (May 1972).

————, "Some Observations on the Economic Framework for Optimum LDC Utilization of Technology," Center Discussion Paper No. 152, Yale University Economic Growth Center (August 1972).

Rotwein, Eugene, "Economic Concentration and Monopoly in Japan," *Journal of Political Economy*, Vol. LXXII, No. 3 (June 1964).

Smith, Edward H., "The Diesel Engine Industry of Daska, Sialkot District," mimeo, U.S. AID Mission to Pakistan (1969).

Sobhan, Rehman, "Strategy for Industrialization in Pakistan," in *Third Five-Year Plan and Other Papers*, Anwar Iqbal Qureshi, ed., Rawalpindi: Pakistan Economic Association, 1965.

Stigler, George J. "Administered Prices and Oligopolistic Inflation," *Journal of Business*, Vol. xxxv, No. 1 (January 1962).

Thomas, Philip S., "Import Licensing and Import Liberalization in Pakistan," *Pakistan Development Review*, Vol. vi, No. 4 (Winter 1966).

Toor, M. A., "Patents as Instruments of the Flow of Technology from Developed to Developing Countries," *Trade and Industry*, Vol. xiv, No. 7-8 (July-August 1970).

Weiss, Leonard, "Average Concentration Ratios and Industrial Performance," *Journal of Industrial Economics*, Vol. xi, No. 3 (July 1963).

Wells, Louis T., Jr., "Economic Man and Engineering Man: Choice of Technology in a Low Wage Country," mimeo, Harvard Development Advisory Service (Cambridge, 1972).

Winston, Gordon C., "Capital Utilization in Economic Development," *Economic Journal*, Vol. lxxxi, No. 1 (March 1971).

————, "Excess Capacity in Underdeveloped Countries: The Pakistan Case," Research Memorandum No. 25, Center for Development Economics, Williams College, Williamstown (September 1968).

Government Publications—Pakistan

Chief Controller, Imports and Exports, *Manual of Imports and Exports Control*, Karachi: 1964.

Controller of Insurance, *Pakistan Insurance Year Book, 1969*, Karachi: 1970.

East Pakistan Industrial Development Corporation, *Annual Reports*, Dacca: various years.

Government of East Pakistan, *Census of Manufacturing Industries in East Pakistan, 1967-68*, mimeo, Dacca: 1971.

Government of Pakistan, Central Statistical Office, *Monthly Statistical Bulletin*, Karachi: monthly.

——, Central Statistical Office, *Pakistan Statistical Year Book*, Karachi: 1970.

——, Central Statistical Office, *Report on Survey of Capacity Utilization by Manufacturing Industries, 1965*, Karachi: 1967.

——, Central Statistical Office, *Summary Findings of the Census of Establishments in Selected Cities, 1962-1966*, Karachi: 1968.

——, Department of Investment, Promotion, and Supplies, *Comprehensive Industrial Investment Schedule for Third Five-Year Plan (1965-70)*.

——, Department of Investment, Promotion, and Supplies, *Directory of Industrial Units Sanctioned During Second Five-Year Plan Period (1960-65)*, Karachi: 1967.

——, Ministry of Finance, *Economic Survey*, Karachi: various years.

——, Ministry of Finance, Central Board of Revenue, *All-Pakistan Income Tax Reports and Returns, 1964-65*, Karachi: 1971.

——, Ministry of Law and Parliamentary Affairs, *Income Tax Act (XI of 1922)*, Karachi: 1970.

——, Ministry of Law and Parliamentary Affairs, *The Tariff Act, 1934* (as modified up to the 31st July, 1968), Karachi: 1969.

——, Planning Commission, *Evaluation of the Third Five-Year Plan (1965-70)*, Islamabad: 1971.

——, Planning Commission, *First Five-Year Plan, 1955-60*, Karachi: 1956.

————, Planning Commission, *Fourth Five-Year Plan, 1970-75*, Karachi: 1970.

————, Planning Commission, *Second Five-Year Plan, 1960-65*, Karachi: 1960.

————, Planning Commission, *Third Five-Year Plan, 1965-70*, Karachi: 1965.

Government of Punjab, *Census of Manufacturing Industries of West Pakistan, 1967-68*, mimeo, Lahore: 1970.

Government of West Pakistan, *Directory of Industrial Establishments in West Pakistan*, Lahore: 1969.

Investment Corporation of Pakistan, *Annual Reports*, Karachi: various years.

National Investment (Unit) Trust, *Directors' Report, 1967-68*, Karachi: 1968.

Pakistan Industrial Credit and Investment Corporation, *Annual Reports*, Karachi: various years.

State Bank of Pakistan, *Balance Sheet Analysis of Joint Stock Companies Listed on the Karachi Stock Exchange, 1964-69*, Karachi: 1971.

————, *Banking Statistics of Pakistan, 1968-69*, Karachi: 1971.

————, *Foreign Liabilities and Assets and Foreign Investments in Pakistan, 1967-69*, Karachi: 1971.

West Pakistan Industrial Development Corporation, *Annual Reports*, Karachi: various years.

Government Publications—United States

U.S. Department of Commerce, Bureau of the Census, *1967 Census of Business*, Retail Trade, Sales Size, Washington, D.C.: 1970.

————, Bureau of the Census, *1967 Census of Manufacturers*, Concentration Ratios in Manufacturing, Parts 1 and 2, Washington, D.C.: 1970 and 1971.

U.S. Department of Commerce, Bureau of the Census, *Population Estimates and Projections*, Series P-25, No. 427, Washington, D.C.: 1969.

U.S. Department of Labor, Bureau of Labor Statistics, *Wholesale Prices and Price Indexes* (August 1967), Washington, D.C.: 1967.

U.S. Federal Trade Commission, *Economic Report on Corporate Mergers*, Washington, D.C.: 1970.

U.S. Senate, Committee on the Judiciary, Subcommittee on Antitrust and Monopoly, *Economic Concentration*, Hearings, Parts 7 and 8, Washington, D.C.: 1968 and 1970.

Index

Library of Congress Cataloging in Publication Data

White, Lawrence J.
 Industrial Concentration and Economic Power
in Pakistan.

  Bibliography: p.
  1. Big business—Pakistan. 2. Industrial organization—
Pakistan. 3. Pakistan—Industries. I. Title.

HD2900.5.W47   338'.09549'1   73-2493
ISBN 0-691-04200-4